"Kelly's book is a significant gift, gather[...] [...]
liance and experience of fellow trave['...] [...]."

—Wm. Paul Young, auth[...] [...]he
[...]k

"Bean has done something of the [...]s
compiled a balanced and informin[...] [...]ensive
guide to today's alternative Christian communities. Even more important
though, it seems to me, is the fact that she has laid open for full scrutiny the
mind-sets, religious perceptions, and soul-filled motivations that undergird
such communities and their individual constituents. Bean's approach, while
admittedly sympathetic, is also born of hard-core, personal experience, and
she speaks with both the integrity and authenticity of one who has suffered
in the course of arriving at her summations and conclusions. I could wish
that every Christian today would read this one."

—**Phyllis Tickle**, author of *The Age of the Spirit*
and *The Great Emergence*

"Kelly Bean is a wise, whimsical, and revolutionary iconoclast. Anyone concerned about the life of the church or the dwindling and precarious role of
Christianity in our culture will find her thoughts sufficiently provocative and
compelling. Her invitation to a non-church faith and faithfulness is a radical
reexamination about what it means to be intentionally oriented to the life of
Christ in community rather than a pattern of church attendance. This book
will call some to leave what is really not church, and it will call others to
reengage the meaning of being a redemptive church."

—**Dan B. Allender**, PhD, professor of counseling psychology
and founding president of The Seattle School
of Theology and Psychology

"Alarming numbers of people are leaving the church. For some this is a loss
to mourn, but for others this represents an amazing opportunity to pursue a
more authentic and embodied faith. I believe our hunger to 'be the church'
and not just 'go to church' reflects a larger shift in our culture toward a more
integral consciousness. In *How to Be a Christian without Going to Church*,
Kelly Bean chronicles the stories of many who have left church institutions
to create new communities of care, spiritual formation, and neighborhood
engagement. Kelly doesn't dwell on what's wrong with more traditional church
expressions or make harsh distinctions between old and new forms. Instead,
she celebrates the possibilities with examples from her own life and the lives
of her global network of friends. She addresses critical questions we should
consider and reminds us that being a Christian without going to church actually requires greater commitment and intentionality. I wish this book could
have been written twenty years ago. It would have saved me from a lot of
frustrated groping in the dark for new alternatives. For those who struggle
with church as they know it, this book can awaken imagination for all that

Christian community can be. Kelly Bean writes with a wise, gentle, honest, and persuasive voice that we should pay attention to."

—**Mark Scandrette,** author of *Free, Practicing the Way of Jesus,* and *Soul Graffiti*

"Despite her provocative title, Kelly Bean loves the church. Indeed, she loves it so much she yearns for it to become more and more the sign, instrument, and foretaste of God's redeeming grace it was intended to be. Packed full of inspiring stories and deep insights, this book will help those struggling to remain in institutional churches, and those who've left, to understand the challenge we all face today and to set some markers for the road ahead."

—**Michael Frost,** author of *Exiles* and *The Road to Missional*

"Some people are leaving traditional Christian congregations to become more faithful and devoted followers of American consumerism. But others are leaving traditional congregations for better, completely unexpected, and wonderfully inspiring reasons. Kelly is the best person I know to tell you about some incredible options."

—**Brian McLaren,** blogger, speaker, author of *We Make the Road by Walking*

"I interact regularly with people of all shapes, sizes, and faith traditions. They love God but have found themselves on the fringes of many church systems. However, their desire for a deep and active faith remains real and strong. In this challenging and engaging book, Kelly Bean acts as an expert guide for exploring the diverse possibilities for living a vibrant Christian faith outside of traditional confines. Filled with real-life stories of creativity, community, hope, and justice, *How to Be a Christian without Going to Church* offers inspiration and ideas that challenge our souls and call us to practice. In a changing landscape of spirituality and church, this book offers a fresh breath of hope and possibility for our future as Christ-followers."

—**Kathy Escobar,** copastor of The Refuge and author of *Down We Go: Living into the Wild Ways of Jesus*

"Being outside the box is overrated. It's inside the box *along the edge* where prophetic leaders do their thing. In this book Kelly Bean has established her credentials as an inside-the-box but along-the-edge leader. From her history with the church, her experience as a leader, her life as a wife and mother, and her journey out of the institutional church, Kelly offers wisdom and guidance. This book is part personal journal, part chronicle of the church in our time, and part spiritual guide. All the way through Kelly is both fair minded and nonreactive toward an institution whose authority she's earned the right to question. Walter Brueggemann is famous for calling prophetic leaders to both critique and energize the church. Without question Kelly Bean is a prophetic leader."

—**Jim Henderson,** coauthor of *Outsider Interviews* and *Jim and Casper Go to Church,* CEO, Jim Henderson Presents

HOW TO BE A CHRISTIAN WITHOUT GOING TO CHURCH

THE UNOFFICIAL GUIDE TO ALTERNATIVE FORMS OF CHRISTIAN COMMUNITY

KELLY BEAN

BakerBooks

a division of Baker Publishing Group
Grand Rapids, Michigan

© 2014 by Kelly Bean

Published by Baker Books
a division of Baker Publishing Group
P.O. Box 6287, Grand Rapids, MI 49516-6287
www.bakerbooks.com

Printed in the United States of America

Library of Congress Cataloging-in-Publication Data
Bean, Kelly, 1961–
    How to be a Christian without going to church : the unofficial guide to
alternative forms of Christian community / Kelly Bean.
        pages cm
    Includes bibliographical references.
    ISBN 978-0-8010-7242-0 (pbk.)
    1. Church attendance. 2. Church. 3. Communities—Religious aspects—
Christianity. I. Title.
    BV652.5.B43 2014
    262—dc23   2014003400

14   15   16   17   18   19   20   7   6   5   4   3   2   1

CONTENTS

Contents

ACKNOWLEDGMENTS

The creation of this book would not have been possible without, first and foremost, the support of my husband, Ken Bean—one of the most patient, dear souls on the planet. I love you, Kenneth. Thanks to my children for stepping up as well during disruptions and prolonged absences for the sake of this book.

Baker editor Chad Allen qualifies as the second most patient person on this planet. Thank you, Chad, for seeing the need for this book and encouraging me kindly for a long, long time. Thanks to Brian McLaren and Jim Henderson for telling me to write and for opening doors. Thanks also to Rebecca Cooper, Brittany Ouchida, Danielle Searl, Molly Kenzler, Stephane Gerhig, and Mary Wenger for your significant roles as editors and readers. You helped bring this book home, and I am grateful.

Thanks to Edie Briggs (the best mom on the planet) and dear friend Gayle Wright—a good share of this book was born in Maui. Thanks to Rich and Joyce Ares—another good portion was born overlooking the ocean at the Oregon Coast. And thanks to Tom and Anita Morgan and Michele Nielsen—a stellar view of Mt. Hood frequently inspired my writing. The creation of this book was made possible because of community.

My Third Saturday Community and Urban Abbey Community have been schools of life and loving, supportive communities through so many stories and through this writing process. I cannot thank each of you friends enough.

Lori Martin, Joyce Ares, and Christine Brunken saved my bacon over and over while I wore too many hats at once. I greatly appreciate the African Road board members and friends who took the work in East Africa to heart while I wrote and helped me carry so many pieces of a newly forming nonprofit in these last years: Susan, Sean, Tom, Dennis, Carol, Timira, Kay, Mary, Bob, Linda, Michael, Marbry, Francine, and Shelley.

Thank you, Marcella Gowan, Adele and Joe Rocket, Jen Lemen, Michele Nielsen, and Michelle Ouchida for believing in me. Thank you, dear friends Molly and Sharon, for faithful prayer and a lot of listening all along the way.

I am blessed with more supportive friends, family members, communities, and networks than I can begin to name in a limited space. Many more of you will find your names and stories in the pages of this book.

INTRODUCTION

Like it or not, change happens. And right now, change is happening in the church.

Longtime members are leaving church. Many young people have little interest in church. A 2005 study conducted by sociologists Kirk Hadaway and Penny Long Marler indicates that fewer than 22 percent of Americans attend a worship service each week.[1] Evangelical pollster George Barna has written about the growing number of people who are leaving church but are not leaving faith. He calls these people "Revolutionaries" and estimates their number at twenty million and growing.[2] David Barrett cites the rise in "churchless Christians" as well, numbering them as 112 million worldwide.[3]

It's well known that the mainline church has been steadily declining in attendance over the last fifty years. Mainline congregations lost between one-fifth and one-third of their membership between 1965 and 1990.[4] And while their decline has not been as pronounced in recent years, it has continued.[5] The steady stream of departures is not limited to mainline Protestant congregations. The Southern Baptist church, "the nation's second largest denomination and long a reliable generator of church growth," reported membership decline in 2011, for the third consecutive year.[6]

Researcher and missiologist Ed Stetzer conducted a study on alternative faith communities in 2008. His research "found that 24.5% of Americans now say their primary form of spiritual nourishment is meeting with a small group of 20 or less people each week." He also notes that six million people in the US attend a small group "and never or rarely go to church," concluding that, indeed, "there is a significant movement happening."[7]

Case in point: Here I am on a bright Sunday morning, curled up in my cushy orange chair, sipping tea and loving Jesus. It's been quite some time since Sunday morning meant getting the whole family spruced up for a church service, racing to get out the door on time, piling in the car, and making the familiar trek to fill our favorite row of seats in a church sanctuary. It's also been awhile since I have chaired a church committee, taught a Sunday school class, preached from a pulpit, coordinated a church potluck, or attended a church prayer meeting.

Back in the day when I was a leader in the churches we attended, we would nod our heads knowingly about the Christians who would darken the door of a church only on Christmas and Easter (we called them "C and E" Christians). We felt confident that those non-churchgoers were not real, committed, growing Christians. And as the times shifted, we began to worry about an increasing cadre of longtime churchgoer friends who were leaving church, never to return.

Funny thing is, now I am one of them, the non-goers. But even still, as a faithful non-goer, I love the church in its various shapes and flavors and would not want to imagine a world without it. Many of my dearest friends are amazing pastors and priests whom I admire a great deal. Let me say right up front, this book is not about the flaws of the traditional church or the pain it can inflict. Those who have lived long in church realize plenty of difficult stories could be told as well as plenty of stories of love, care, compassion, commitment, and community. But this book is not about those stories either. This book is about those times when, places where, and people for whom attending organized "church" does not work. People may not participate in church for a season or even for the long haul for numerous reasons. I know I am not alone in my experience. This continues to be confirmed over and over as I meet more and more creative and proactive non-goers.

In 2006, I sat on a stage at an Off the Map Live event with pollster George Barna to participate in a panel discussion on changes in the church. Barna is the premier expert in the study of the relationship between evangelical religious belief, behavior, faith, and culture in America. While he's been far more devoted and committed to the church in America than most of us, in more recent years he has been on an unexpected excursion out of the institutional church. In his quiet but confident voice, Barna explained how he was led to employ his professional expertise in polling and statistics to help examine his own growing unease with church. His research showed "a radical gap between what we heard Christians professing they believed and the values and the lifestyle that grew out of the values."[8]

As he began to look for alternatives to church as he'd known it, Barna experienced a burst of growth in his faith and a new sense of purpose. He found this energy as he engaged in Christian community outside of the institutional church. The hope and excitement Barna experienced led him to write his book *Revolution*. In *Revolution*, Barna delves into his discoveries and shares his perspective, both of which led him to the belief that the answer to the disappointment he was experiencing with church and what he saw as dismal results of the work of the church is to be found in small home communities.

A few years ago I sat in a small group with theologian Walter Brueggemann. He leaned forward and fixed his piercing eyes on us as he declared that Christian community must begin to offer the world a prophetic counter-narrative through Scripture, a narrative that frees people from a "script" that leads to oppressive ways of living. These changing times call us to birth prophetic communities of Jesus followers who are not driven by self-ambition or by desire for personal comfort but who are in touch with God's heart of healing, reconciliation, and redemption for all the world.

Presently, both the Internet and a greater sense of global community bring a new set of considerations to the table. We are keenly aware, as never before, how interconnected we are to each other and with the rest of the world. The Internet provides a whole new political theatre with real-life players. Both the Internet and our sense of connection to each other are significant for non-goers who want to be part of healing and reconciliation in this world. Some might scoff and doubt that real connection can take place virtually, but many will tell you otherwise—including me.

The Internet can be used to find and get to know new friends, network with people who have common interests, share prayer requests, communicate and learn from people of other faiths, share and get ideas for mission or problem solving, encourage people who are isolated, spark revolutions (as powerfully evidenced in the Arab Spring uprisings), raise funds for a well in Africa—or a friend with cancer, or for legal fees, or for a neighbor in need—learn of a new book, find out when and where a speaker is coming to town, or learn about and arrange meet-ups with other small groups of non-goers you wouldn't have met otherwise.

Frankly, the possibilities for goodness that can be generated via Facebook, Twitter, blogs, online fund-raising platforms, and email alone are flabbergasting. Used well, the Internet and social media hold the potential for moving us far beyond communication to real connection with others. For those who are being Christian without going to church, the Internet throws the door wide open for creating new types of community of faith and practice.

As a person who led and served in church for more than two decades, I know the importance of gathering together as the visible body of Christ and encouraging each other to practice love and do good deeds. Now, as a non-goer and cultivator in an ever-evolving Christian community, I also believe there are healthy, visible, doable alternatives to the traditional church. Becoming a non-goer does not have to lead to waning faith or cynicism but instead can lead to a life-giving, world-changing, growth-inducing, community-building way of being.

As you read this book, I invite you to meet friends of mine. I hope you will be encouraged by their ideas, projects, and stories. Their lives are being lived in so many active, committed, Jesus-loving, world-serving, gathering, and worshipful ways. I invite you into my own stories to see how God has been at work through both good times and difficult times. Life as a non-goer calls on our courage and creativity. It's not handed to us or periodically attended. It's not to be taken lightly or attempted alone. You will have to reach and try, find and connect, risk and learn. But if you are faithful to the Spirit within, the wisdom of community, the best of the long-lived, life-giving traditions of the church—and if you do not go it alone—you will find your way.

I welcome your own experiences, doubts, feelings, and hopes—whatever they are. This book title may stir enthusiasm in you, or it may raise concern. When I made the title public, a friend and respected mentor who faithfully follows her call to pastor a congregation through thick and thin was honest enough to let me know the title hurt. You might have such feelings too. My friend knew me well enough to know my life and to know that my intention was not to undermine her or the church, but still, she had feelings. That is fair. Last year I was invited to speak at a popular Christian conference on the topic of leadership in small faith communities. When the conveners saw this book title in the bio they requested for their print material, they quickly sent a note retracting their invitation, explaining that the book was a problem for them. I am okay with that.

At the same time, I have now lost count of how many people, when they heard this book title, have taken an involuntary gasp as though they have felt a blast of fresh air. They may exclaim, "Wow! I want to read that!" or "Thank you for writing this book. I left the church to preserve my faith. Maybe you understand." While I hope this book assists you along the way, I believe the truest guide, no matter whether one is "going" to church or "not going" to church, is the Holy Spirit, our companion, who has begun in us a good work and will not leave us now.

Whether you are a new non-goer, a longtime non-goer, or you are wondering about those who are non-goers—whoever you are and wherever you find yourself—welcome.

You are not alone!

Part 1

THE BIG SHIFT—FROM GOING TO BEING

THE BACKSTORY

Confessions of an Amateur Church Anthropologist

This book was born out of my experiences as a leader in church and as a non-goer. My own story of church began when I was a child, and even before in the stories of my grandparents. My life today, my non-goer status, and my call to lead are all woven of experience. I didn't just wake up one day and decide to become a non-goer. It may help you to be introduced to that story as we begin to explore the non-goer phenomenon together.

My Formative Years

I have been something of a church anthropologist since the age of three. Church runs in my veins, and there is no getting past it—I have been shaped and formed by the church. My grandfather on my dad's side of the family spent his life serving as a minister in rural Methodist churches up and down the West Coast. My mom's great-grandfather was a Presbyterian minister in the late 1800s to a congregation in what was then the wild, Wild West town of Baker City, Oregon.

In my own lifetime, I've been given plenty of opportunity to "study" church in a variety of contexts. My parents claimed Christianity when they encountered Jesus through Campus Crusade for Christ when I was a young child. They did not share the devotion to denomination their forebearers had, but instead they sought a variety of experiences, visiting one form of church after another. We moved a number of times in my childhood, and every time we moved we'd try out a new "flavor" of church. We attended the Congregational Church, the First Baptist Church, the First Christian Church, the Presbyterian Church, the Wesleyan Methodist Church, the Covenant Church, the Lutheran Church, and the American Baptist Church.

In addition to our regular church attendance, my parents took my three younger sisters and me on weekly "family field trips" to check out other worship gatherings.[1] These ranged from Faith Center, a charismatic Foursquare congregation in Eugene, Oregon, to hippie worship gatherings on rickety old front porches in 1970s Jesus People communes. We attended energetic Sunday night services at Bible Temple, a growing Pentecostal mega-church in Portland, Oregon, where people marched down to the front of the sanctuary to deposit their weekly tithes and offerings (much to my discomfort as an introspective introvert). Our curious white faces stood out in the warm, welcoming congregation of Maranatha, a vibrant inner-city black church. We joined crowds at Kathryn Kuhlman healing services in auditoriums and Billy Graham crusades in stadiums. We went to Pat Boone concerts, where we checked out his classic white buck shoes, and we clapped and swayed at groovin' Andraé Crouch gospel concerts. This meant that for well over a decade I attended evangelical church services and Christian gatherings of nearly all types at least several times a week.

As I began middle school, we entered the Lutheran Church phase. I discovered that it had something new to me: liturgy.

In my own quiet way, I loved it. We stayed long enough for me to memorize and deeply digest the liturgy and to go through confirmation classes. Martin Luther made an impression on me, and I was eager to be confirmed into the church. The sanctuary was a beautifully rendered, partially round, contemporary design constructed from Pacific Northwest timbers with a breathtaking, soaring ceiling, arched beams, clerestory windows high above, and seating curving around the open altar. I was nourished as I soaked in the symbolism of the architecture and the rhythm and theology of the liturgy.

I might mention that I was a true dreamer from an early age. I sometimes dreamed of a faith community that could incorporate the best of these expressions—beautiful meeting places, whether the warmth of an old front porch or a thoughtfully designed room, peaceful presence, multicultural and intergenerational participation, the wisdom and rhythm of liturgy, soulful singing, thought-provoking theology, heartfelt laughter, good food, people who really knew and helped each other in practical ways, joy, hope. And even at that young age, I knew I could do without the offering plate marches, prayers demanding God do what we ask, long sermons, artificial hospitality, perky singing, simple answers, and exclusion I had sometimes witnessed. When I reflect on this preteen chapter in my spiritual life, I realize how much I was formed then and how it still shapes my practices and preferences as a non-goer today.

Then it was on to the American Baptist chapter.[2] My relationship with the American Baptist Church was a "chapter" rather than a phase because it stuck for a long time. When I was in the eighth grade, my family began to attend a particular American Baptist church that was something of an anomaly because it was charismatic. I learned the praise choruses, became familiar with the culture, and observed people enjoying the active community life of this large, thriving congregation.

Real Life in the Church

Several years after high school, I returned home from college and met the dashing Ken Bean, a handsome and kind motorcycle-riding youth group leader at the same charismatic American Baptist church. We eventually married and settled into making a life as "grown-ups" in this church. I plunged in with earnest intent and participated in all the offerings for young married women. We started a family and began to host a small Bible study/fellowship group in our home.

Over time, though, I became discontented; I sensed that God was so much larger than the limitations, politics, and theology represented by the church I knew. At an annual church business meeting, I noticed that the salary of the woman who was the children's minister was only a fraction of what was made by the young man who was the youth pastor, although she often put in double the hours.

When I asked about this, I was told that it was expected that her husband would be the main provider for the family. This both startled me and awoke something in me. I began to notice who held visible positions in the church and think about the reasons why. For the first time I began to notice that women served only in support roles or in positions leading other women or children, and that there were no women on the elder board. Rarely did a woman stand behind the pulpit for any purpose except to lead a song or make an announcement. I began to get in touch with how it felt to be marginalized. That led to noticing others who were excluded, and I began to wonder if this was what Jesus had in mind.

It is worth noting that God can use discontentment partnered with prayer and exploration to usher in change more than one might expect. In response to my discontentment, a wise mentor—incidentally the first woman pastor I'd ever known—scratched out a Scripture verse on a bit of paper and suggested that I post it somewhere I'd see it frequently: "If from there you seek the LORD your God, you will find God if you seek God with all your heart and with all your soul."[3]

I took this advice to heart and began to study Scripture and theology on my own. This verse rekindled my dreamer spirit. I was encouraged; my questions were valid, not heretical, and by golly, there were other ways of faithfully understanding Scripture than ones I had been taught. As my internal questions grew stronger, so did my faith and my sense that God was far, far larger than the narrow confines I sometimes felt in church. In the meantime, although the church we were part of did not authorize women in leadership, I had moved naturally from the role of host for a small group in our home to leadership in one of the fastest-growing and vital small groups in the church.

After seventeen years in this church I'd grown up in and married in, my husband and I joined a new church plant born out of the American Baptist Church. The house group followed suit and continued on together, growing into "a church within a church." This was the place where I was really known and accepted. And it was the place where I helped create space for others to be really known and accepted.

As active lay leaders, my husband and I began to have growing concerns about what we considered to be misuse of pastoral power in this young church plant. We spent several years seeking and working for healthy solutions with the leadership team. In the end, the pastor did not welcome the perspective of the lay leaders and asked the leadership team to resign. After twelve years of life as part of this church family, we finally made the difficult decision to leave.

As I look back, I can see how I was formed for the better by sticking it out through painful times, learning through each step of the process, choosing to forgive when offended, creating safe space for others along the way, valuing relationship, and giving grace as freely as I'd like to receive it. In doing so, I encountered Christ in a deeper way and discovered the value of being empowered without disempowering others.

I can also see times I judged too quickly, acted without full knowledge, and sometimes reached the wrong conclusions. Coming to terms with my own failures in the story forms me and humbles me as much as the virtuous path of patience and forgiveness. Yet, in leaving we did what we needed to do, and in the leaving, new doors opened.

Arms Wide Open[4]

Somewhere in the middle of all this, I began making weekly treks to the Benedictine Abbey at Mt. Angel near my home. I also added occasional visits to an assortment of Episcopal services, where I could soak up the liturgy. At the abbey I met a Christ who understood suffering—a Jesus who was a great relief and comfort. No matter what my lot was, this Jesus was there to companion me rather than fix me and shine me up. An unspoken expectation that I had picked up along the way in life was that, as a good Christian, I should get it together, be good, and look good. This image was replaced by a Jesus who knew pain and whose own life looked messy at times. This Jesus was present, and even at work in mysterious ways through the painful disappointments and dark nights that real life inevitably holds.

Now mind you, I'm grateful that this crucified Jesus is also a resurrected Jesus, changing the course of history through his ultimate redemptive act with resurrection power and hope. I sure wouldn't want to live a joyless life devoid of hope. It's just that the traditions of my childhood emphasized a jolly Easter morning Jesus in a way that discouraged honesty about showing real feelings if they weren't pretty and seemed to deny that good Christians might struggle at times. I needed the balance of knowing Jesus as the One who is wholly present even when the night is long. I needed to know that all my feelings were of value and that wearing a happy mask was not the way we were intended to live with God or others. Whew!

Both at the abbey and in the Anglican Church, where I sometimes slipped into the back row, the strong traditions and the cycles of the church calendar gave me a sense of peace. I relaxed into the well-traveled patterns of ancient Christian faith. Sister Antoinette, an elderly, wise Benedictine nun, became my spiritual director. She led me into the legacy of prayer practices that had been followed by devoted Christians for ages: Lectio Divina, centering prayer, and fixed-hour prayer. These practices led me ever closer to Jesus, helped to sustain me through crisis, and strengthened me for the demands of day-to-day life.

As my view of Christendom expanded, so did my faith and my curiosity. I began to earnestly seek expressions of Christian faith that could be more relevant to those people I'd mused about for many years, the ones outside the church. In doing so, I discovered that many others like me were exploring faith and following Jesus in the swirling postmodern context of today's world—people who were keenly aware that the times were changing and who didn't want to miss out on what God is doing in this time and place. I began to read paradigm-shifting ideas: teaching through story, living incarnationally (in ways that follow the example of God, who came into the world to identify with us and be with us) and missionally (rather than trying to bring others to us, we go to others and participate with God in what God is already doing in the world), valuing the ordinary, and re-envisioning doubt and uncertainty as a normal part of the Christian walk. I learned of artists who were finding their place in the church for the first time. I was inspired by countless conversations and by witnessing living examples of uplifting ways to follow Jesus.

Another powerful and instructive shift for me came as I encountered Trinitarian theology. This profound, relational understanding of God is intrinsic to ancient Orthodox theology and practice. Although the idea of "Father, Son, and Spirit—Three in One" is understood to be an essential doctrine in most churches, the way each was portrayed in my experience of church made them seem as though they are very separate beings. *The Icon of the Trinity*, painted in 1410 by Russian artist Andrei Rublev, captured me: three graceful figures with identical faces and physiques are dressed in flowing robes and seated congenially around a table.[5]

For me, the power and beauty of the Rublev icon is the co-equal depiction of the members of the Holy Trinity—they sit together in a circle of interactive relationship. I began to ponder the implications of a God who was not a lone deity bossing people around, a Jesus who was not an underling, and a Holy Spirit who did not just go around doing odd things on her own. Rather, a new idea emerged. Trinity: God who exists only in community; God who is with us. With this in mind, God no longer seemed to be a disparate, hierarchical trio but instead a community within Godself, who is always in corresponding relationship. This sort of understanding of God means that autocratic forms of leadership aren't very godlike; lonely sacrificial life isn't really what it's about. Experience with God always points us to relationship and community with others.

I began weaving all these new ideas and ways of being into my weekly community gathering—sharing books, resources, thoughts and practice, hopes and dreams.

By now, the group that was my faith community had become home to not only the cadre of longtime faithful members but to an assortment of artists and creative thinkers with their own gifts to share. Although the congregation this group had been born out of sadly did not continue, this little faith community was alive and well, meeting in our home and growing strong. I thoroughly enjoyed the process of noticing what others could bring to community and creating space for them to do so. This was at the heart of what it meant for me to lead in a way that felt natural, though it was not a style that had been modeled for me. Down the road I would begin to encounter others who were leading this way and would forge new friendships within what would be sometimes called the "emerging church." There I would find my gifts and my call recognized and welcomed.

Now, clearly serving as the pastor of a faith community, I felt the tug to enter seminary to continue to learn and explore. And nearly twenty years after its inauspicious start, this weekly church home group evolved into Third Saturday Community.

The childhood "church anthropology" project has expanded in scope beyond my imagination. When I look back over my story thus far and see the ways God has shaped and formed me through the experiences of life, through many nontraditional and nonacademic arenas (as well as through seminary and the study of scholarly works from wise Christians who have gone before me), I catch my breath in wonder.

In all these contexts it has been my hope and aim to, in some small way, bless the church and her leaders. Along the way I have formed close friendships with amazing pastors, ministers, and priests who are faithfully leading their congregants toward Jesus and whose work and call I esteem highly. I love the deep wells of Christian history and tradition. I have been drawn to cultivate leaders and build leadership networks, and I have faithfully served the church for many years. Even so, it is interesting that now, years after leaving our church plant, although not for lack of trying, my family has not found a church tradition and congregation to call our home. It seems that our organic communities, with no paid staff, no worship team, no association to denomination or particular tradition, have become the laboratories of love and relationship where I, as part of a living and growing community, learn how to be a Christian without going to church.

I write this book with a desire to see a world changed for the better as people practice "being Christian" together in ways that birth faithful communities, spur generosity, encourage kindness, and inspire the hard work of reconciliation on the home front and in the world. I believe living into these practices will translate into action that provides food for the hungry and healing for hearts and bodies—and kindles a passion for justice in the systems and structures that shape this world. I am aware of the ways I fail to live this way daily, and at the same time I am keenly aware of the Jesus who redeems all things, including my stumbling attempts. I believe it is as we faithfully practice and stumble along together that we meet Christ.

When I reflect on the timely words from Scripture given to me twenty years ago as my guide for a journey into the unknown—"If from there you seek the LORD your God, you will find God if you seek God with all your heart and with all your soul"[6]—I marvel at the unexpected and incredible ways I have come to and continue to find God. It is out of this life experience that I write this book. I write as a learner, an amateur anthropologist of experience, an ordinary person who loves Jesus, and a leader with a hopeful heart. Times are changing and, to no surprise, God is up to something interesting.

Questions and Action

1. How has God used your history and experiences to shape you?
2. Have you experienced a variety of Christian traditions and denominations? What unique strengths did you find in each?
3. Where were you in life when you first sensed the connection between God and community?
4. Can you relate to the idea of discontentment ushering in positive change?

2

WHAT THE HECK IS CHURCH?

The Church in All Its Forms

Church.

That one small word is power-packed with meaning. To help unpack that power, I started asking this question of people: "What first comes to your mind when you hear the word *church*?"

This is what I heard: "My mother wishes I would go." "Singing." "Run!" (Interestingly, this response was from a pastor.) "Boring." "Sermon." "Sunday school." "Life." "Dead." "Family." "Power." "Potluck." "Money." "Pastor Tim." "Friends." "Confusing." "Love." "God." With so much variety in church experience, it is no wonder that responses to the word *church* vary so much. These replies do raise questions for us. What is church? Is the church today what it was intended to be?

To know what it might mean to "be the church," it's first important to take a look at what Scripture, history, and the example of Christ teach us about church and its purpose.

Touring Churches

We often use language about church in a way that conditions our thinking—church becomes a place to go, something to attend, an event to plan, a program to consume or critique, or a ministry identified by the personality of the pastor when, in fact, the church is a people to be. Although most people understand church is much more than a place, event, ministry, or dynamic leader, those ways of thinking hold a great deal of power. They influence us more than we may realize.

Listen to yourself talk about church and see what you notice. Since I began to think about this book, I noticed my own habits don't always represent my theological understanding of the church. For instance, last week I suggested to my family that we might go visit "Pastor Deborah's church" (emphasis on the leader). In arranging a meeting, I suggested that we should meet at a church (emphasis on the building). I recently heard that a young friend was attending church services for the first time in his life. I asked him, "Scott, where are you going to church?" (emphasis on the weekly event).

Argh. Old habits die hard. These uses of the word *church* are fairly harmless, but they do serve to reinforce ways of thinking that detach us from remembering that we are not called to go to church, think the church belongs to the pastor, or serve a building. We are called to *be* the church.

A congregation in the Portland area, Bridge City Community Church, addressed this well by intentionally naming their building and encouraging the congregation to refer to the building by name: the Bridge House. This reinforces the fact that the structure is merely a container for the community. Rather than saying, "Let's paint the church blue," they would say, "Let's paint the Bridge House blue." These simple shifts in language can help to recondition our thinking and remind us what church is and what church isn't.

Ecclesiology, Scripture, and history all challenge the deeply engrained message of what it means to go to church. First of all, it is helpful to be reminded that the term "church" has been used in a multitude of ways and has no direct biblical source. Instead, it is the Greek word *ekklesia*, or "called out ones," describing something more than an assembly, that we find in the New Testament. The two Scripture verses where Jesus uses this word, Matthew 16:18 and 18:17, have been translated to read "church," losing something of the meaning of *ekklesia* in translation. The word *church*, from the middle English *chirche*, was derived from *kiriakon*, meaning "house of the lord" (small *l*).

This term for house of the lord originally referred to the house of an aristocratic guy with knee socks, not to a house for God. But *chirche* did come to be known as a house for God. When we start building houses we hope can contain God, we miss the point. That all ended when the temple veil was torn in two. God made it clear that God could be accessed by anyone—without a priest and without a special building. Christ was God with us and we were with God. Houses of worship can remind us of God, be places of creative beauty that inspire awe and reverence, be used to honor God, and certainly serve the *ekklesia*. At their best, they can serve the surrounding community. Yet they cannot contain God.

This linguistic lesson expands rather than diminishes our understanding of what church means and can be. I would not want to imagine a world without a visible church. I would not want to be without the rich traditions and rituals of the church. I would not want to discourage anyone from being part of church, and I would not want to encourage people to go it alone in their faith. What I do want is to reexamine our understanding of church in light of the increasing number of non-goers in the Western world. I want to faithfully re-imagine what it means to be a Christian in this unique time in history.

My friend Jim Henderson, a devoted Christ follower, former pastor, and the founder of Off the Map, took an unusual tour of the country with his friend Matt Casper. Matt describes himself as an atheist with an open mind. As they traveled, they visited a variety of church congregations to get Matt's take on different forms of church. *Jim and Casper Go to Church* is the insightful and refreshing book they wrote as a result. As a newbie to the customs of church forms, Matt's experience of church led him to ask this worthy question: "Is this what Jesus told you guys to do?"[1]

Jesus didn't leave instructions that paint a picture of a particular structure. The Bible offers us the image of Christ's body having many parts. Jesus builds close relationships and makes disciples. He hangs out with poor people and sick people, with women and children and lepers, and despised people—he is drawn to people who are on the margins of society. He looks for humble hearts, he rests and he eats, he heals when the need for healing shows up, he breaks bread and shares wine and invites us to "do this in remembrance of me."[2] He lays down his life for others, and he brings hope.

Jesus spent most of his time with a small group of disciples. To follow his example means that Christians will care about making and equipping disciples who will take positive action in the world. Pastor and author Brian McLaren calls this "disciple-formation and disciple-deployment."[3] Like Christ's early followers, as we gather and follow in the good news of his ways, we discover that his presence is with us and we go forward to be people who bring good news. As Jesus promised, "Where two or three gather in my name, there I am with them."[4]

Leonard Sweet and Frank Viola put it this way in their book *Jesus Manifesto*: "What is Christianity? It is Christ. Nothing more. Nothing less. Christianity is not an ideology or a philosophy. Neither is it a new type of morality, social ethic, or worldview. Christianity is the 'good news' that beauty, truth, and goodness are found in a person. And true humanity and community are founded on and experienced by connection to that person."[5]

Richard Rohr, a Franciscan priest whose work I admire a great deal, fills this picture in a little more:

> It's true that the church did not officially start until the Day of Pentecost, but since the church is based on the person and work of Christ, it really began with Jesus. He is the one who is "calling out" people who will call upon Him for salvation. All who do so are automatically members of the body of Christ through the baptism of the Holy Spirit (see 1 Cor. 12:13). When it comes to the church, there is the church invisible, comprised by all those who have trusted Jesus as Savior and Lord. And there is the visible church, comprised of those who gather together. Not all members of the visible church belong to the body of Christ, and not all who belong to the body of Christ gather physically in a church.[6]

Not long after the time Christ walked this earth and his immediate followers experienced his presence in powerful ways, the church settled in and became an institution. The institution has done a great deal of good over the centuries, and it still does. At the same time, the structure can lack the flexibility to respond aptly to the times and can sometimes be a barrier to growth and healthy change. Rohr offers this challenging observation of both the Protestant and Roman Catholic traditions:

> Historically, religion has more often been a belonging system or a belief system, than an actual system of transformation. When belonging and believing is your primary concern, you do not really need healing or growth, or even basic spiritual curiosity. All your homework is done for you and handed to you. If you let the group substitute for your own inner life or your own prayer journey, all you need to do is attend. Church for several centuries now has largely been a matter of attendance at a service, not an observably different lifestyle. Membership requirements predominated, not the "change your life" message that Jesus so clearly preached. Membership questions become an endless argument about

who is in and who is out, who is right and who is wrong? Who is worthy of our God and who is not? This appeals very much to our ego, and its need to feel worthy, to feel superior, to be a part of a group that defines itself by exclusion. The Country Club instinct, you might say. That is most of religious history. The group's rightness or superiority becomes a convenient substitute for knowing anything to be true for oneself. Where did Jesus recommend this pattern? It has left Christian countries not appreciably different than other countries, in fact, sometimes worse. The two World Wars emerged within and between Christian countries. We can do so much better.[7]

In a commencement address given at the Virginia Theological School, my friend Brian McLaren reminded the graduates that:

The church doesn't exist to satisfy the religious tastes of its members. Nor does it exist for institutional self-preservation. Nor does it exist to provide clergy with fulfilling employment and generous remuneration and an unparalleled retirement package. But rather it exists to join God in God's self-giving for the sake of the world. As the church moves beyond a season of internal tension and conflict, this is a prime time to focus on our dual mission of disciple-formation and disciple-deployment into the needs and un-seized potentials around us.[8]

McLaren is hopeful that the church can and will move beyond "internal tension and conflict," and I am too. Many churches, to their credit, are indeed grappling to understand what God is doing and how to respond accordingly and focus on the "un-seized potentials" of this time.

Signs of Changing Times

The power and influence of rapidly changing technology shapes us in ways nothing ever has before. Never before have people been so interconnected across the planet and across belief systems. Never before have we had access to so much information instantly available at our fingertips. The significance of this unprecedented shift in history cannot be underestimated. For non-goers, technological advances open up potential for new communities and connections that didn't even exist in the imagination twenty years ago. Clearly, the shifts we are experiencing cannot be dismissed as just another round of the next generation and its latest passing trends.

It's one thing to talk about technological trends. It is another to consider what the deeper ramifications of these changing times are for the church, the people for whom church exists, and the people who have left the church. After talking with hundreds of people and reading reams of research, I'd venture to say that people leave church (or never come to begin with) not so much over matters of style, cultural relevance, or the lack of the latest high tech trends. These aren't inherently bad things, and in fact, depending on the context, they may be good things.

But these may not be the kinds of changes needed to draw people toward a growing faith, into the life of being a Christian in such a way that changes not only their own life but makes the world a better place. While a focus on trends and style can be a distraction from the invitation "to join God in God's self-giving for the sake of the world," understanding how people process information and becoming aware of the sort of community people are hungry for in this technology-saturated time is important. It's a new world, and we must learn how to navigate in it.

I know there is a good case to be made for the role of institutions. Evergreen Community Church of Portland, Oregon, meets in the Lucky Lab Pub on Sunday mornings. Bob Hyatt, planting pastor of Evergreen, makes this point: "To say, 'I don't need to be part of a local church because I AM the church' is like a football player standing alone on the field saying I AM the team. It's silly." When asked about "leavers," he assigns blame to church communities who refuse to grow past religion into real mission and relevance.

It is good to note evidence that some churches are showing a desire to respond to the changing times. My friends Angie Fadel and Geoffrey Neill co-pastor The Bridge PDX (not to be confused with Bridge City also in the Portland metro area, pastored by another friend). The Bridge meets in a yoga studio, composes original music for their worship gatherings, operates on a shoestring budget, and tends to draw people from the artist community, the streets, and the Portland alternative music scene. The Bridge provides a place that makes sense to these people and is a place they meet Christ and feel a sense of family. The music is raw and honest. Children join in all aspects of the gathering as they choose. All the same, the traditional structure you might expect in most any church service—a sermon, announcements, a music worship segment, a closing prayer, and a clear start and end time—knits it together.

With Evergreen's pub meeting place and The Bridge PDX's yoga salon home, these churches are working out what their neighborhoods may need. Northwest Church Planting, located just across town in a gritty area of Northeast Portland, has been influential in coaching church leaders around the Pacific Northwest to lead their congregations in considering healthy reproduction more important than growing in size. As a result, many new churches have been given a great start with financial, emotional, spiritual, and mentoring support from mother churches. In an effort to reach more people, some churches have chosen to form multi-church sites as a solution for stretching resources, sharing leadership, and building a broad base in multiple neighborhoods. Some stream live sermons from a main campus while others operate elsewhere with a smaller staff supported by the vision and administration of the main campus. House churches and the emerging church movement all indicate that people and churches are aware of and searching for something more, something other than what has been.

In addition to technological and cultural changes, economic changes have affected the church. In 2008, the national and global economies began to slip quickly into the worst economic downturn since the Great Depression. This destabilization added urgency to a factor that was already a consideration for many in the church as well as for many outside of the church—sustainability. As unemployment rose and home owners faced losing first their savings and then their homes, charitable giving and tithing dropped dramatically. Church budgets plummeted, church staff had to be cut back, and church members felt pressure on all fronts. As fuel prices rose, people began to think twice before driving any distance. Large suburban commuter churches felt a pinch they had not felt before.

Poverty in the suburbs is becoming a more pressing issue and requires a response. People have an increased awareness of the need to live in ways that are local and sustainable. This awareness carries over to what they want and need in church as well. This time in history presents both challenges and opportunities to the institutional church and to followers of Jesus. The times really are changing, and whether or not she is ready, this is a point of change for the church.

I am right there with Bob Hyatt: we were not made to go it alone, and the body of Christ cannot be the body of Christ if we give up on each other. But what happens when the structures, institutions, and forms that exist now—even innovative new forms—are no longer working for a growing number of people? New questions become important. How could structures of human relationship be shaped today? How can faithful non-goers be the church? What might new communities of believers look like? How do we equip those who are new to the faith? What the heck does the world need the church to be in this time?

I do not pretend that the way forward is easy or simple. Fact is, most of us are joiners, glad to be part of a group and generally content to stay the same instead of opening ourselves to transformation. Ryan Sharp of the band The Cobalt Season rightly observes that "moderated community is easier than creating direct community." He adds, "The hope of moderated community is that it will lead to un-moderated relationships. If, however, it [church as moderated community] dissolves, often the relationships do as well. Still, we don't all want to make all the decisions. We want trusted gate-keepers. Someone invented a T-shirt. I don't want to get up every day and have to invent what I wear."[9]

It is true that being church takes a lot of work and a lot of time. But growing numbers of people are ready. They are done just joining; they have become non-goers who are heeding a call to go and be in new ways. Hyatt suggests that churches can bear more responsibility for leading congregations into real mission and relevance. I think he's right. Some will and some do. In the meantime, though, there will still be leavers. A growing cadre of committed non-goers are hearing a call that is at once new and at the same time ancient—the call of the Spirit.

It is my observation and my ongoing hope that even for non-goers, history, tradition, theology, and doctrine will serve as gatekeepers and guides. The intent isn't to abandon the larger story. We are all part of an old tale that has been unfolding, not just since Pentecost but since the beginning of time. Our story has markers and traditions that knit us together and remind us who we are. We don't want to lose that perspective. We are here at this point in history because of the people who have gone before us, good and imperfect people like us to whom we are humbly indebted. Stories and traditions are containers to help carry us forward as we are part of the continuous story of church history. The stories we create now will inform the generations who are coming up after us and those who are already disenfranchised, watching from the sidelines.

The great news is that it is possible to be a Christian and not *go to church* but by *being the church* remain true to the call of Christ. The following chapters explore what is behind the growing phenomenon of non-goers and the possibilities of small, humble groups of people following the person of Jesus, being formed and transformed together and, as a natural result, walking with, eating with, and serving a world hungry for hope.

⟫ Questions and Action ⟨

1. What comes to mind when you first hear the word *church*?
2. What do you notice about your own linguistic use of the word *church* after reading the observations on the various uses/meanings of the word *church* in this chapter?
3. How has technology changed your own life and the world around you, particularly spiritually?
4. Are you in any ways indebted to the historical church or traditions of church?

3

WHY ARE PEOPLE LEAVING?

The World Keeps Turning

A recent smattering of books has begun to take serious note of the exodus from church. *Revolution* by George Barna, *Quitting Church* by Julia Duin, *unChristian* by David Kinnaman and Gabe Lyons, and *You Lost Me* by David Kinnaman with Aly Hawkins plumb reasons people are leaving church or have no interest in church to begin with. The European church has led the way in "leavership" and in forging innovative, alternative faith communities for some time now. *The Post-Evangelical* by Dave Tomlinson of the UK explores what is taking place in this context.

Barna's single solution is house churches. Ms. Duin harkens back to the days of the Jesus People movement in the '70s for inspiration but generally doesn't note many promising trends now. Kinnaman offers a razor-sharp, statistically based analysis of how young people perceive the church and Christians, which leaves us to wonder where to go now. Jim Henderson's *The Resignation of Eve*, backed by statistics from the Barna Group, contends that women are leading the way out of the evangelical church because of its limits on leadership for women. Dr. Alan Jamieson, a pastor in New Zealand, spent six years documenting the accounts of what he describes as church "leavers." His book *A Churchless Faith: Faith Journeys beyond the Churches* is one of the most comprehensive studies of people leaving evangelical, charismatic, and Pentecostal churches. Jamieson describes "a steady stream of people who were leaving churches . . . when they felt they could no longer stay and continue to develop in their Christian faith."[1] The trend goes beyond evangelical and charismatic churches. Diana Butler Bass, a respected author and scholar of the mainline church, documents in *Christianity After Religion: The End of Church and the Birth of a New Spiritual Awakening* a general shift and dissatisfaction from all corners of Christendom.

It is clear that many are on their way out, and for a wide variety of reasons. Not only am I one of these statistics, but I know many other people who at one time were committed to a traditional church and now no longer are. The sum of these stories and statistics makes it clear that we must pay attention.

Munching on tasty turkey sandwiches in Seattle, Washington, David Kinnaman, coauthor of *unChristian* and *You Lost Me*, and I shared tales of the complexities and joys of parenting, then moved from talking about families to talk of faith communities and on to the fascinating research project David had completed as he wrote *unChristian* with coauthor Gabe Lyons.

Lyons's work with young people across the country prompted him to approach his friend Kinnaman in hopes of investigating and then making known the growing, not-so-flattering perception of Christians held by many sixteen- to twenty-nine-year-olds (both churched and unchurched) in the Western world today. Kinnaman caught the vision and off they went. The news they returned with is not encouraging. "Young outsiders and Christians alike do not want a cheap, ordinary or insignificant life, but their vision of present-day Christianity is just that—superficial, antagonistic, depressing. . . . [If we do not respond now] we will have missed our chance to bring a deep spiritual awakening to a new generation."[2] These are words to heed as we consider the future of how Christianity itself is being represented to and perceived by an increasingly post-church generation. I would add that it isn't only young people who perceive the church and Christianity in this light. A growing number of non-goers of all ages may not have ditched faith, but often they too identify with these sentiments about church and Christians as a group.

Friends Who Left

People become non-goers for many different reasons. The following stories share experiences and developments of friends who have left church. You may see yourself or someone you know reflected in these accounts. While we are each shaped in unique ways and have our own stories, you may discover kindred spirits in these pages. It is also possible that you may hear ideas and questions that are new to you. Whatever the case, my hope is that you will be encouraged to continue to learn and grow in faith and in connection with others around you.

Roger, Barb, and Julia

It was a bright but chilly winter morning. I climbed aboard a TriMet bus for a ride into downtown Portland and plopped myself down in one of the few remaining vacant seats. My seatmate was hidden behind the morning paper. I duly pulled out my current read and buried my nose as well. A few miles down the road, the paper reader folded up the news. I was startled to discover that I was sitting next to an old family friend, one who'd been an influential mentor to my husband and an elder in the charismatic American Baptist church we attended for some years. Roger and I proceeded to become regular seatmates and enjoyed catching up in brief installments on our rides into Portland.

One of the bits of news Roger shared was that he and his dear wife, Barb, had recently enjoyed dinner with Julia Duin, a woman who, when in her early twenties, had lived with their family. I remembered Julia as a slender and serious, harp-playing, clog-dancing church member. Julia, it seemed, had gone on to become an accomplished journalist and author. When Roger mentioned that she had been a religion writer for the *Washington Times*, the pieces fell into place. I had occasionally read Julia's column but hadn't previously identified her as the thoughtful young harpist from years ago. It turns out that Julia had also written a book, published by Baker Books. This book happened to be called *Quitting Church*, an interesting discovery in light of my work on this book in progress.

Roger proceeded to share that after forty-plus years in church leadership, he and Barb no longer attended church. "Has your faith been shaken?" I asked. "No, not at all," replied Roger. They had simply grown discouraged with church politics. After one last crushing disappointment, they'd thrown in the towel. Roger told me how much they missed being part of an intergencrational community. Their grandchildren lived out of the area, and the friends Roger and Barb occasionally gathered with for prayer and fellowship now were all older. The connection with the younger generation had been one very important part of church life for them.

I sympathized and asked Roger if he would reintroduce me to Julia. Within a few days I'd purchased and read Julia's book and was in email communication with her. In *Quitting Church*, she frequently harkens back to that American Baptist church of our youth. She does not mention the church by name, but her depiction rings true enough that I can easily recognize it. Her recollections are a good deal more nostalgic than mine, but they are astute all the same.

Duin traces her trek after leaving the Portland area. She tried church after church, facing repeated difficulty as she tried to find an authentic community where she, as a single woman with a career, could fit in. Although I was a bit young to access this at its peak, Duin's most significant experience of authentic Christian community took place in the heady days of the 1970s Jesus People movement in the community of that American Baptist church. Nothing she has encountered since then has matched that experience. Duin makes the connection between her disappointing experiences in attempts to find a welcoming church that has solid teaching and a healthy community life with the experiences of growing numbers of people who are vacating church around the country.[3]

Roger and Barb ultimately left church because of the limitations and power structures of the church they were part of. Interesting to note, as a longtime elder, Roger himself had at one point been part of that same power structure, the one that kept women, young people, and others in the margins, out of leadership. After many years, Roger and Barb asked themselves the same question Matt Casper asked of Jim: "Is this what Jesus told you to do?"

The answer that eventually came clear to Roger and Barb was no, it wasn't, and they left. Leaving meant losing friends of many years and losing the regular interaction with the younger generation they loved. Becoming non-goers was no small sacrifice, but the structure they were part of was killing their faith and their hope. They had to.

Julia continued to face the obstacle that woke me up years ago back in the church we'd both been part of—the marginalization of those who don't meet certain criteria. As a brilliant journalist, a religion writer with a keen eye on current events, and a devoted mom, over and over she found herself frustrated with the difficulty of finding a church where she could fit in and where she was welcomed and valued for who she is. Years of faith in Christ and a passion to live a life that counts still guide them. Roger, Barb, and Julia haven't given up, but their stories look much different than they might have ever imagined.[4]

Edie and Gayle

Edie, my perky seventy-eight-year-old mom, began attending church when she was twenty-one years old. She taught Sunday school, tithed faithfully, attended women's Bible studies, and served on hospitality teams and women's ministry committees for forty-four years. A decade ago she just stopped going. Now she and her best friend, Gayle, spend their Sunday mornings hosting brunches and blessing people in their neighborhood by installing drip water systems in flower gardens up and down the street. Their neighbors know who they are and what they would do for them. I asked Gayle and Mom why they left and how it has been for them since.

Mom admitted that after a near half-century of serving on committees and work groups, she was tired out and had come to feel undervalued. "I spent all my time with Christians and I worked hard for the church. There was a time when that was fun, but after a while I started to notice that women weren't really seen as valuable contributors in my church. We did the work but our opinion wasn't welcome. Our work wasn't even valued in the budget or church calendar. That was when it started to feel tiring. My faith is as strong as ever. I pray. I still connect with other Christians—those I can relate to spiritually. I meet with these friends a couple of times a week.

"And I have so much more time. Now I spend more time with non-Christians than I did in my whole life. When I do something to help people now, I know that the giving comes from my heart and that it really blesses the person. That is exciting. Knowing this ignites my spirit and expresses my faith in real ways. Some Christians spend all their time at church and don't even know their neighbors. Gayle and I know all our neighbors and they know we care about them. Our next-door neighbor found out that he had prostate cancer. He told us before he told his family. His wife called us right after the surgery, before they called the family. That is sacred stuff."

I asked if her old friends wonder about her non-goer ways. "It's true. Every time I run into someone I went to church with all those years, one of the first things they ask is, 'Where do you go to church?' I just say, 'I don't.' They really don't know what to say. They are always shocked. It is sort of sad. People make assumptions."[5]

Gayle joined in. "I haven't missed church—sometimes I miss singing in a large group, and I've lost track of some friendships because we don't see each other every week. Overall though, the purpose of why we gathered got lost in the corporate structure. My experience is that my church became more about human plans, budgets, and control than about meeting people's needs and serving the world. The leaders had too much power and too much control. Men didn't value women. Older leaders didn't value younger leaders with new vision. An organizational psychologist once spoke at a conference I attended for work. Her words really stuck with me. She said that whenever you have more than two people working together on anything there are only two ways things can function—they will either be a team or a gang. They will work for the whole or take what they want. I saw trusted church leadership function like a gang. It killed it for me. Watch out for gang activity! I can say that my friend Carren pastors a church that I admire. She works very, very hard to build a team."

I asked Gayle what her thoughts were about life since she became a non-goer. "You know, I have had so much more relationship with non-believers since I left church than when I was in church. I am impressed and reminded of the grandeur of God when I hear stories of God at work in the world. God is not bound by the institution of the church. I say serve others, let your life speak, and follow Jesus with whatever it is you are passionate about."[6]

Jim

Jim Henderson used to be a pastor. He planted churches, led worship, performed weddings, launched evangelistic campaigns, led small churches and was on staff at a mega-church, preached scores of sermons, and did all the right pastor-y things for twenty-five years. Then he stopped. For the past seventeen years, he and his wife, Barb, have been non-goers. Jim now leads the production company Jim Henderson Presents, and produces thought-provoking events designed to help people explore the connection between faith and action.

I asked Jim why he quit initially. Here's what he said: "I was on staff at a mega-church. The same problems of staff drama and politics that I'd seen for years in smaller churches were magnified. The system that we inherited for doing church is broken and we have just adjusted to it. The power of the institution reigns and can bring out the worst in humans. For me, trying to go to church and just sit there knowing how poorly the staff was cared for caused terrible dissonance. I'd stand in the parking lot and watch hundreds of cars line up to go in and out. I realized that although the system is broken, it doesn't matter to most people that it is broken. When I recognized that, I knew that I was done."

Jim experienced deeper growth after he left church than when he was part of and even leading a congregation. "After seventeen years of not going to church, my faith is stronger than ever. For me, [being a non-goer] removed the obstacle of dissonance between what the church could be and the dysfunction inherent to the institution. [Being a non-goer] forces me to think more deeply about why I do what I do and why I don't do what I don't do. If you are just reactive, then you won't grow. But if you are reflective, you will keep growing. That is my story."[7]

Jim is not alone. Hundreds and hundreds are asking good questions and then choosing to leave. I wondered what Jim thought about the other reasons people are leaving church.

"Church has come to mean a church service or event," he said. "Churches have organized around a church service as their identity. That takes away 90 percent of the rich identity and intention of the church. I can tell you, services will become boring and predictable—you can only entertain people so long.

"Also, right now the world is going through huge changes in communication and technological advances that are shifting the ways people think, connect, and learn. Cultural changes and the complexity of life are causing people to think twice about how they spend their time and what they commit to. While culture is changing rapidly, what is slow to change is leadership awareness. We are still using the same leadership model as pharaohs—oligarchy when the people have made the shift to charting their own course in a people's sort of polygarchy. People don't have the same amount of time they used to, and they don't feel as inclined to give loyalty to institutions as they once did. People don't feel guilty and obligated in the same way they used to. When middle adopters, the more conservative people (not just hippies, artists, and nonconformists), start to abandon ship, you know something is up."

Jim continued, "Some people leave because they mature and graduate. I think there are stages of life in church. One of the problems of church is that it is parental—with leaders directing and telling people what to do. What happens when people don't need that anymore?"

Despite his non-goer status, Jim has a soft spot for leaders in the church and often refers people to churches led by his friends. "I don't want to have to go to church, but I care about, respect, and admire people who are leading. I am glad to help them. And I am still grateful that I have a place to send people. I think most people need a structure and a ritual. I guess I don't need to be reminded that I need to follow Jesus. I think about it every few minutes."

I wondered how people handle the idea of a pastor who no longer goes to church. Jim explained: "At first I went to a church service about once a month. Really that is all you have to do to make people happy. That works to keep a public person in good standing. You can say you attend a particular church and people will be satisfied. But really, do you think Jesus wants us to be that way? Eventually I started doing what I wanted to do. I stopped going. I think I've established my credibility over the years. I think people now just give me a weird pass."

Jim and Barbara met over forty years ago when Barb was a young nun. There is a story there, but it is one to be told by them. Barb has gracefully managed many years of serving in Protestant, mostly charismatic churches since then. She has successfully merged that life with her strong Roman Catholic background. Sometime after leaving church, she wrote an ingenious little book called *Simple Spirituality*, patterned after the small groups she has led for years. The book and the small groups focus on seven core beliefs and seven corresponding internal practices. Here they are in a nutshell:

1. God is good. I will practice trusting God with my life.
2. God is love. I will practice taking care of myself and loving others.
3. God is with me. I will practice peace and not being afraid.
4. God wants to talk with me. I will practice listening to Him and talking with Him.
5. God always forgives. I will practice forgiving myself and others.
6. I feel blessed with this Good News. I will practice being thankful and celebrating moments.
7. God has a story of love, He tells it through us. I will practice partnering with Him to bring it to others.[8]

Jim told me that most mornings he and Barb recite the first three points before beginning their day. Barb spends her life on others, caring for the elderly, the mentally ill, the vulnerable. She loves Jesus and she doesn't miss church life at all.

Joyce

When as a teenager she became pregnant, my sister-in-law Joyce, an honors student, made the choice to marry the father of her baby. For years she navigated a difficult marriage. When she decided she could no longer live within an abusive marriage, she faced rejection and judgment from church and, more specifically, from the people in it, including church leaders. That was when she made the decision to continue her faith and leave the building behind.

Whatever remaining points of contact she had with church left her with a sense that she did not fit in and was not respected for the strong woman she was. Joyce didn't abandon the deep faith of her childhood and young adulthood. She still misses the hymns of her childhood church, she prays and asks God for guidance, she knows Jesus. But instead of finding her place inside the walls of a church, she has given herself to community service. Joyce—brilliant, warm, and dynamic—has invested years helping to shape her neighborhood, city, and county through roles in county government, and with dedicated service on boards of education, political advocacy, and public education campaigns. In addition, she is a wonderful mother and grandmother. Her children and grandchildren seek her out for wise counsel, which is well seasoned with experience and grace. Joyce's faith paired with her personal experience of facing hardship motivated her to get involved right where she lived and to make a difference. In doing so she has influenced many people and made her community a better place for all people to live.

It's interesting to me that Edie, Gayle, Jim, and Joyce range in age from fifty-nine to seventy-eight years old. They are people of mature faith and perspective, yet their views and their real-life experience in church are remarkably similar to that of the young people surveyed by Kinnaman and Lyons. Whether we see through the lens of experienced non-goers or we view Christianity and church through the eyes of young people in America today who will shape our world tomorrow, we may find views that are remarkably similar and quite instructive to anyone seeking to understand how to go forward in these changing times. We can learn from people of all ages and a wide variety of experience.

I know the young leaders who meet with me for mentoring often teach me more than I teach them. I also learn from a wide assortment of incredible twentysomethings who hang out in my living room to talk, nap, and eat. I have known many of these gifted young artists, musicians, thinkers, and activists since before they could walk. They encourage me and help me to better understand and engage with the world. I am thankful for these friends. One young friend is a Christian who does not go to church. She is also the daughter of a well-known pastor (a very kind, wise pastor, I might add). I'll call her Amy.

Amy

Amy shared with me what she thinks about being a Christian without going to church. Her values (which are strongly shared values for many other young people who have left church) of authenticity, meaningful engagement, welcoming space for all, creativity, real-life connection, and a faith that motivates people to change the world are clear in her hopeful and charitable perspective.

I think the problem with church is that somehow the message is that going to church every Sunday is supposed to help you feel that you really are a Christian. If you do find a church that works for you, I think this is wonderful. But driving around just about any town or city I see tons of churches that simply don't match my style with their cheesy postings 'CH_ _CH, what's missing? U R.' This makes me think of small talk, polite smiles, and the occasional donuts and coffee . . . it's all pleasant and welcoming in a very organized and packaged way. But I don't think it helps me be a Christian. It is sort of like going to your grandma's house and talking about half the things going on in your life to keep things simple and smooth. With certain environments and certain people, you have to adopt a certain code of how to act . . . it's completely unspoken but it happens.

I think that being a Christian is real when you can be who you are as an individual. See what you have to offer the world. Work with your friends to create environments that welcome people. Thank God this *can* happen. Forming communities outside of church is safe, and scary, and completely worth it. There is absolutely no reason to believe this is any less important than going to church, nor is there any reason to feel that your faith is any less valid than someone who practices their faith in a more traditional setting.[9]

Non-goers of all ages want real relationships and real experiences. Many times they have not found these or seen these modeled in the institution of church. If we choose to be involved somewhere, we want it to be a place where we can be authentic and both contribute and receive. We want relationships without pretense. We need room for doubt and questions and acceptance rather than rejection.

Dannika

A blog post written by college student Dannika Nash captured the strong sentiments of many young people today. Nash's post, written after attending a concert by the band Macklemore, struck a positive nerve with thousands on the Internet and Facebook. Macklemore's hit song "Same Love" is practically an anthem for young people across the country. Listen up to Dannika's "An Open Letter to the Church from My Generation." Whether or not you agree with her, her words are instructive for anyone who is trying to understand some of the reasons people are leaving church. Dannika presents us with a matter of significant concern, especially to young people today. Here's an excerpt:

> My point in writing this isn't to protect gay people. Things are changing—the world is becoming a safer place for my gay friends. They're going to get equal rights. I'm writing this because I'm worried about the safety of the Church. The Church keeps scratching its head, wondering why 70% of 23–30 year-olds who were brought up in church leave. I'm going to offer a pretty candid answer why, and it's going to make some people upset, but I care about the Church too much to be quiet. . . . Lots of things in culture are absolutely contradictory to love and equality, and we should be battling those things. The way culture treats women, or pornography? Get AT that, church. I'll be right there with you. But my generation, the generation that can smell bullsh–t, especially holy bullsh–t, from a mile away, will not stick around to see the church fight gay marriage against our better judgment. It's my generation who is overwhelmingly supporting marriage equality, and Church, as a young person and as a theologian, it is not in your best interest to give them that ultimatum.
>
> My whole life, I've been told again and again that Christianity is not conducive with homosexuality. It just doesn't work out. I was forced to choose between the love I had for my gay friends and so-called Biblical authority. I chose gay people, and I'm willing to wager I'm not the only one. I said, "If the Bible really says this about gay people, I'm not too keen on trusting what it says about God." And I left my church. It has only been lately that I have seen evidence that the Bible could be saying something completely different about love and equality. . . .
>
> It's hard to hear about love from a God who doesn't love our gay friends (and we all have gay friends). Help us find love in the church before we look for it outside. . . .
>
> Love,
> A College Kid Who Misses You.[10]

A *Los Angeles Times* article backs up Dannika's perspective, shedding more light on young people who are finding themselves disaffected from church: "According to a mounting body of evidence, [a predominant reason young people are leaving the church is] politics. Very few . . . actually call themselves atheists, and many have rather conventional beliefs about God and theology. But they have been alienated from organized religion by its increasingly conservative politics."[11] We can see these common themes in Amy's thoughts and Dannika's blog post. Sometimes people, young and not so young, become non-goers when those they care about are not welcome or when they perceive the church valuing political positions more than acceptance and welcome.

Wisdom from Across the Pond and Down Under

The United Kingdom, with only 14 percent of one thousand people surveyed in 2010 saying they attended church at least once a month, is also the soil where early creative, alternative Christian communities began to flourish.[12] People who were done with the church but still looking for a way forward began to explore possibilities together.

Dave and Pat Tomlinson (davetomlinson.co.uk) started a gathering in a London pub in 1989. At that time the notion of using such a venue to bring people together to talk about Jesus and life was practically unheard of. The Tomlinsons did so with a keen awareness of factors that alienate people from the church. The structures of the church were often seen as restrictive and disconnected from real life. While people might not have had interest in church membership or in attending church, they did have a genuine hunger for exploration of faith, spirituality, and Christianity. This pub community came to be known as Holy Joes and led the way in innovation that gave hope to others who had departed church.

In his book *The Post-Evangelical*, Dave Tomlinson expressed the sentiments of people drawn to Holy Joes. Their experience of churches with "more literalistic interpretation of scripture . . . allow[ed] little space for the insights of critical approaches to exegesis." He continued, "Dependence on an uncritical reading of the Bible as external authority in matters of belief and ethics" was one significant factor in departures from the church.[13] The shopworn phrase "God said it, I believe it, and that settles it" doesn't leave much room for honest exploration of Scripture, theology, and real life. Holy Joes made room for lively intellectual and spiritual honesty and for exploration of dogma and doctrine in light of lived experience.

As I looked at research about people leaving church, I encountered the work of Alan Jamieson, a pastor from New Zealand whose research I mentioned earlier in this chapter. He observed growing numbers of faithful people leaving church in his context. In response, he wrote the book *The Churchless Faith* as his doctoral dissertation. His academic research primarily considers Evangelical, Pentecostal, and Charismatic populations, which he refers to as EPC. Jamieson uses four categories to identify non-goers who have left church but not left faith.

1. "Disillusioned Followers" leave because they are hurt or angry or they have come to disapprove of the leaders or vision of the church. They hold firm to EPC biblical interpretation and practices, at least initially.[14]

2. "Reflective Exiles" leave not because of hurt but because they are re-evaluating and deconstructing foundational questions of faith, beliefs, values, and blind acceptance of a leader. They often begin to wonder about biblical models for church and have "ideas for a new way of church."[15] They are often, but not always, challenged to reevaluate core beliefs after facing difficult life circumstances. Disillusioned Followers may become Reflective Exiles.

3. "Transitional Explorers" focus not on what they have left but on beginning to find a new way forward. They are "reconstructing" rather than deconstructing.[16] Reflective Exiles may move forward to become Transitional Explorers.

4. "Integrated Wayfinders" have gone through a process of evaluating Scripture and previously held beliefs. Often they have embraced the possibility that there is truth in other belief systems and certainly in other expressions of Christianity than their former EPC context. These non-goers are "more accepting, less defensive and more willing to enter into open discussion."[17] Worship, meals, work, sexuality, finances, relationships, service, emotional life, and creativity all become deeply connected to faith and integrated. Integrated Wayfinders have a new willingness to use their time, energy, skills, and resources in pursuit of their faith. For them Christian service flows out of deep spirituality. They have found a way forward. Not all Transitional Explorers become Integrated Wayfinders, but many do.[18]

A good deal of the study and research regarding people leaving the church in North America today considers young people or explores the decline of the mainline church. What is interesting to me is that most of the non-goers Jamieson studies and interviews are like Edie, Gayle, Jim, and Joyce— seasoned Christians who do not represent a young demographic. They are not uninvolved, are not mainline, are not leaving faith, and are not likely to return to an EPC church. They are solid, longtime churchgoers with strong faith.[19] One Transitional Explorer puts it this way: "Don't tell me I pulled out because I was backsliding. It is because of the spiritual side of me that I pulled out."[20] Jamieson's respondents often expressed that there was no way for them to move forward within the structure due to paternal leadership models that don't provide a path for people as they spiritually mature. "EPC-type churches are strong on evangelism but comparatively weak in their emphasis on faith maturation."[21]

My friend Arnie was raised Mennonite, married Sharon, a good Catholic girl, and met up with Jesus through the Catholic charismatic movement. Over the years, he and Sharon helped to plant a church and went on to serve as key lay leaders in small and large congregations for decades. Today they spend their time mentoring, counseling, and praying for scores of people who are interested in growing in faith and personal development. It has been ten years since Arnie was a member of a church congregation, but he shared this discovery with me: "I have learned and grown more in ten years than I did in decades of going to church."[22] Both Arnie and Jim each shared their experiences of more growth and maturation outside of the structures of the church than they'd gained inside those structures. I was interested to read psychologist David Benner's work on this topic. Benner explores the process of transformation and growth from the perspective of faith and psychology in his book *Spirituality and the Awakening Self: The Sacred Journey of Transformation.* From Benner's perspective, when an evolving community isn't available, then leaving could be considered a natural and expected outcome of growth. He writes, "Sometimes transition out of a community that is providing more constraint than support for our growth is difficult—on occasions, even traumatic. Other transitions are smoother. And a fortunate few find themselves in a community that evolves as they evolve."[23]

Wisdom from the Third World

This phenomena of leaving church, being Christian but not going to church, and being spiritual but not religious, is generally more common in the Western world and Anglo-Eurocentric contexts than elsewhere. Although this book explores the culture that has shaped me, it is no secret that the church is booming in third world countries, growing in astronomical numbers. In his book *The Next Christendom: The Coming of Global Christianity*, author Philip Jenkins documents this veritable explosion. We cannot and should not ignore the unique ways God is moving in other cultures around the world and in immigrant communities in the United States.[24]

Dr. Soong-Chan Rah's *The Next Evangelicalism: Freeing the Church from Western Cultural Captivity* challenges the white Western church to become aware of how evangelicalism has been held captive by its predominantly white cultural identity and history. He rightly suggests that immigrant, ethnic, and multiethnic churches are better prepared to adapt to the complexities and realities of this time than the individualistic and materialistic Western and American churches.[25]

Time writer Elizabeth Dias explores the rapidly growing Hispanic church in America. She explains that "The evangélico boom is inextricably linked to the immigrant experience. Evangélicos are socially more conservative than Hispanics generally, but they are quicker to fight for social justice than their white brethren are. They are eager to believe in the miraculous but also much more willing to bend ecclesiastical rules."[26] My friend Liz Rios is a dynamic Latina pastor in Florida. Her growing church and ministry is an illustration of this side of the changing face of the church in America.

Before we know it, Asia, Latin America, and Africa will send more missionaries to the Western world than we send out. At the same time, as Dr. Soong-Chan Rah makes clear, sisters and brothers of color here in this country could become our sage guides for the way forward—if we open ourselves to learn.

Unexpected Hope

There are many stories to learn from. People leave church for plenty of other reasons as well. In a July 31, 2013, Facebook post, church historian Diana Butler Bass responded to the social media fervor over a CNN article by blogger Rachel Held Evans called "Why Are Millennials Leaving the Church?" Looking through the lens of history and statistics, and bristling a bit, Bass posited that millennials leaving church is a matter of "exponential demographics."

Throughout the last 100 years, there has been a steady increase in the number of people who dis-affiliate in each generation. With each increase, it is like multiplication, not addition. The millennials' parents and grandparents "left" at a rate of about 15%. Those people married other people who also left religion. They had unaffiliated children. Those unaffiliated children married and had the second generation of unaffiliated children. Because there are more of them, they have wider cultural influence and converted their peers. So, the millennial unaffiliated rate is double that of a generation (or two) ago. This pattern began in the 1920s—and was obscured for about 20 years immediately following WWII—and the trickle turned into a stream turned into a river.

It is always wise to look at the larger picture, and Bass makes a good point. When we add the factor of exponential demographics to the plethora of stories and statistical research that track church attendance and public sentiment about church, we see an extensive and complex set of reasons for an increase in non-goers. Time pressures and life priorities challenge us all. Young families and single-parent families are stretched by the demands of raising children. Singles are deluged with more choices for the use of their time than ever. Two-income households are reluctant to give up time for something that does not seem to impart significant benefit or have real meaning. An aging population faces health and mobility issues. The effort it takes for overcommitted, overextended people to get to a ninety-minute service or give time to programs and church events can be too much. Sometimes staying home on a Sunday morning seems like the best way to remain sane.

No matter the reason—the pressure of time and life commitments, discouragement over disempowering leadership structures, a desire to be more connected to local events and neighbors, or the constraints of rigid theology or political perspectives; a lack of value for the gifts and perspective of all in the congregation, a process of spiritual growth that moves you to "graduate" (true as this can be, watch out for the pride factor here—sometimes good graduation candidates are able to choose to stay to nurture others), or a rejection after a significant life change or a personal failing; a culture of pretense and too-niceness, a longing for a more integrated lifestyle, the injustice of discriminatory practices, or the desire for freedom from social pressure to attend church; or a longing for more authenticity, a value for a more sustainable way of life, or new ideas about what church could or should be—people are leaving something they have known and loved. People are leaving church. They are stepping out into the great unknown of how to be a Christian without going to church. If you see yourself in these stories, remember Arnie's heartening observation that he has grown more in ten years outside of the church structure than in decades in church. In the chapters to come you will find stories of others who have gone forward to create meaningful post-church community.

⟫ Questions and Action ⟪

1. Can you relate to any of the stories in this chapter?
2. What do you think about the idea of Christians maturing and graduating?
3. What do you think about the idea of churches evolving to make a place for maturing Christians?
4. If you are a non-goer, do you see yourself in one of Jamieson's categories (Disillusioned, Reflective, Transitional, Integrated)?
5. What feelings does this chapter bring up for you? Fear? Excitement? Anger? Fatigue? Relief? Hope? Other?

Part 2

EXPRESSIONS OF FAITH

WHAT ARE THEY DOING NOW?

The Call of the Wild Goose

People may be leaving church congregations, but often they are moving toward something rather than moving away from something. What is drawing and calling people of faith as they leave church? This chapter explores what the Spirit may be up to in today's world.

Longing for More

Some have left the faith, some are drifting, and some may be lapping up the luxury of fewer commitments and taking in the *Sunday Times*. Yet many others are finding new ways to live out their Christian faith, still adhering to an orthodox faith while finding new, imaginative forms of expression and practice. While many left because of dissatisfaction and disconnection with traditional church involvement, when they find alternative communities of Jesus they are energized to reengage. Communities that facilitate genuine relationships and provide room to participate in meaningful ways can re-kindle the desire to orient their lives around God's work in the world.

This is the category of non-goers that Alan Jamieson calls Integrated Wayfinders. They are the ones who, after leaving, find themselves with "a new willingness to use their time, energy, skills, and resources in pursuit of their faith."[1] Their faith is not held in one compartment of their lives but weaves seamlessly throughout the details and experiences of life, from the most menial to the most meaningful. This kind of integration requires honest and authentic companions for the journey. It takes time, vulnerability, and a high level of commitment. Yet the authenticity of their faith expression makes that level of commitment sustainable. Jamieson found that for these people, faith after becoming a non-goer is "held to even more tightly and with higher degrees of commitment than in their time in their church days."[2]

This way of living out faith can lead to more cohesive and sustainable ways of being than we find in the fractured and demanding lives many of us lead. Women's group Monday night, choir practice and youth group on Wednesdays, Dinner for Eight group on Friday, Sunday school Sunday morning, Sunday service, Sunday evening mission committee and prayer meetings—the list can go on. Certainly, each of these opportunities in their own right can facilitate community and provide meaningful engagement, but sometimes the busyness of involvement in church activities brings disintegration and distraction too. Activity can, at times, come to stand as an impressive-looking substitute for an authentic faith.

Wild Goose

When I can nudge my sedentary self off the leopard-print couch I use for a work station, I get my blood circulating by pedaling my blue bike up the steep hill out of my neighbor-hood. My first destination is the grassy open space belonging to Marylhurst University. There, flocks of wild Canada Geese honk and flap furiously to make themselves known. They are vocal and fearless, occasionally traipsing together en masse into the middle of the highway that runs alongside the field to hold a group protest. Seeing them I am reminded of why the early Celtic Christians chose the image of the wild goose to represent the Holy Spirit. This powerful, raucous, feisty, messy, beautiful bird is an apt symbol for the shift in the church today. A new wind is blowing, the Wild Goose is calling, and people are following.

The Iona Christian Community in Scotland uses the wild goose as a symbol for their community. An annual gathering of Christians in the US, patterned after the Greenbelt Festival, a creative Christian arts and worship gathering in the UK, has chosen to go by the name of Wild Goose Festival, harkening the same symbolism. Although wild geese aren't always predictable, they aren't loners either. Geese fly much faster when they fly in formation than alone. One goose will lead the formation, and when that goose tires it drops back and the next one in formation assumes the lead, and so it goes on through the ranks. This prevents burnout, keeps them all on course, and keeps them all in fit condition. Increasingly, collaborative and non-hierarchical leadership is a hallmark of many of the emerging faith expressions. This seems to be more and more the way of the Spirit in this time.

Non-goers may be charting new territory in their expressions of faith, but like the wild goose they are seldom going it alone. Freedom of expression and room for questions and difference are common values for these non-goers. Instead of plunging into profound individualism and smorgasbord spirituality, they draw from the narrative of Scripture and the wells of tradition, and they seek balance and companionship for the journey. These non-goers are likely to look for faith expressions that support integration of ordinary life, authentic relational community, hands-on engagement, and smaller, more sustainable forms of community.

In his book *Post-Modern Pilgrims*, author and lecturer Leonard Sweet identifies a cultural shift from the preferred value of individualism to the increased longing for community. Sweet explains that our culture is drawn to what he calls EPIC, an acronym representing the value for Experiential truth and Participatory engagement, Image-Driven meaning, and is all about being relationally Connected.

Experiential: This culture is not interested in attaching to or debating beliefs. Sweet declares that people today "don't want their information straight. They want it laced with experience."[3] He says, "Truth resides in doings as much as documents."[4] The bottom line is that people are hungry not for information, apologetics, or rules but for their own spiritual experience.

Participatory: Interactive, two-way engagement is important to people in this culture. They value experience, but it doesn't stop there—they want to be part of shaping the experience they have.

Image-driven: Sweet writes, "Images generate emotions, and people will respond to their feelings."[5] This culture "is image driven. The modern world was word based . . . Images come as close as human beings will get to a universal language."[6] Visible examples of the Good News being lived out are needed more than ever at this time in history.

Connected: "The pursuit of individualism has led us to this place of hunger for connectedness to communities, not of blood or nation, but of choice."[7] When it comes to discovering or teaching truth, we need to be aware that at this time in history, "Truth resides in relationships, not documents or principles . . . Not until the fourteenth century (at the earliest) did truth become embedded in propositions and positions."[8]

Sweet is right when he tells us that in the modern world the common assumption was, "I think, therefore I am."[9] Today, the longing for deeper connectivity and meaningful relationship has taken us another direction—back to an ancient sensibility. Bishop Desmond Tutu describes this sensibility well, using the African concept of Ubuntu (meaning, "I am because we are"). "A person is a person through other persons . . . we are made for a delicate network of relationships, of interdependence."[10] Indeed, this is what we long for and as non-goers can work to create together.

America, in particular, historically heralds the rough and rugged individual who beats the odds, conquers the wilderness, and goes it alone. But the luster of this narrative is fast fading in recent decades. The EPIC shift from a "me" to a "we" is evident in the world today.[11] A desire for communal action and renewal is rising. I wonder, could the Wild Goose be stirring a new contingent, the committed non-goers, who will be part of new stories worth telling for generations to come? What might be possible with a group of people who seek to follow the Wild Goose together, committed to let the Good News permeate all areas of life and to carry a blessing into the fabric of their own neighborhoods and ordinary lives?

Many non-goers are leaving the institutional church in hopes of finding something more than what the structures in which they had been a part could provide or allow. They are engaging in age-old practices that are new to them (often adopting ancient Christian practices or lifestyles), and they are cultivating relationships with intention. They are caring for their neighbors and keeping it simple and real. These people want to make a difference in the world and in their communities. Rather than focusing on programs, curriculum, excellence, and performance, they are doing what is doable right in their own backyards while some are being stirred to sacrificial action in response to profound needs in other parts of the world. They are practicing being disciples and inviting others to a winsome way of discipleship.

The Wild Goose is present in the longing for *Experience* that is real and honest, in hands-on *Participation* rather than observation, in visible, concrete *Images* of the living gospel, and in ordinary, authentic, relational *Connection* between human beings. Although these non-goers value experience and relationship, ultimately their desire is to be spiritually formed and to follow in the way of Jesus and the relational God who exists in the shape and community of the Trinity.

Non-Going Spiritual but Not Religious Folks

In this post-church generation, a growing number of people consider themselves "spiritual but not religious" (SBNR). This phrase can mean an assortment of things. It is not at all uncommon to find people who attend church regularly who say they are spiritual but not religious. It is very common, especially in the Pacific Northwest where I live, to meet people who would never go to church but strongly identify as spiritual but not religious. While being spiritual but not religious isn't synonymous with being a non-goer or with being a Christian, it is true that many people who follow Jesus and are now non-goers do think of themselves this way. My non-goer friend Michael, a poet and brilliant tech guy, resonates with both SBNR folks and with his Christian heritage. He describes himself as "spiritual *and* religious." I like that.

When I think of being spiritual, I think of encounters with a sense of the transcendent and the divine when I am out in nature. For me there is nothing like the purifying, powerful beauty of the Pacific Ocean on the Oregon coastline. I feel cleansed after a long afternoon walking quiet beaches. It offers me a sense of coming close to God. As an introverted child, I felt safe and companioned reading books in the arms of an ancient tree. When I look back, I can see this is one way I experienced God early in my life. Whether it's beholding majestic mountains, taking in wide-open, sage-fresh, starlit desertscapes, exploring the marvels of a garden, or holding a newborn baby, you probably have had moments like this too.

People who identify themselves primarily as being "religious" sometimes equate being "spiritual" with Western and American self-absorption and individualism and may dismiss it as willy-nilly New Age thinking. But for those who identify themselves as "spiritual," the word represents a way of life that isn't fettered by rituals, rules, and beliefs that feel irrelevant. It is relational and vibrant. In her book *Christianity After Religion*, religion scholar Diana Butler Bass notes that "In the United States, some 30% of adults consider themselves 'spiritual but not religious.' . . . To say that one is 'spiritual but not religious' or 'spiritual and religious' is often a way of saying, 'I am dissatisfied with the way things are, and I want to find a new way of connecting with God, my neighbor and my own life.'"[12] While adherence to a specific set of beliefs is unlikely to be of great importance, commitment to regular practice is often a high priority. In a recent Huffington Post article, Philip Goldberg wrote this about spiritual but not religious folks:

> I would wager that, on average, they [SBNR people] spend far more time in meditation, prayer, study of sacred texts, devotional activities, group discussions and other actual practices than the conventionally religious. Let's face it, a large percentage of people who call themselves religious engage their faith for a couple of hours a week at most, and many only on holidays. As someone once said, sitting in church and thinking you're spiritual is like sitting in a garage and thinking you're a car.[13]

An archived "Spiritual but Not Religious" website (SBNR. org) puts it this way:

> Spirituality draws me deeper into the moment. It is the experience, inspiration and awareness that evoke meaning, connections and the rapture of life. Spirituality is humanity that is experienced deeply. It is real. It is fun. It is practical. It is joy. It is pain. It is extraordinarily ordinary.[14]

I can hear the cry of the Wild Goose in these words. This SBNR definition moves from solitary experience to one of community and connection. For non-goers, who follow Christ but have left the traditional structure behind, finding and creating human community of some sort is essential for growth and for engaging in the call to be bearers of the Good News in the world. Along with my deep connection to creation and the natural world, I have found that when I take the risk to experience God in real human community, I am most challenged to grow and change. Psychologist David Benner puts it like this: "Commitment and continuing quest develop within an interpersonal context, and the journey that they lead to, if it is to result in transformation, will always unfold within and between communities of others who either facilitate or impede awakening and unfolding."[15]

Whether it starts with finding a connection to God in the sunset, taking notice of the ordinary miracles of each day, making a way forward with new, growing communities of connection, or joining together for action that brings transformation to neighborhoods and streets, something is going on outside the walls of churches that is worth sitting up and taking note of. More than ever, the world needs to see lived communal examples of what it means to be Christian. This is the time for non-goers to explore the possibilities as they are stirred by the spirit of the Wild Goose.

The Tradition of Change

When we step back and look at the big picture of church and at the growing phenomenon of non-going, it is possible to discern larger historical shifts at play. Taking a look at our cultural setting isn't pandering to cultural relevance and accommodation. In fact, when we seek perspective, we are following a biblical example. First Chronicles 12:32 tells us that the people of Issachar "understood the times and knew what Israel should do." Because they were paying attention to their cultural and historical situation and were aware of their place in it, they had a sense of the way forward. It may be comforting to remember that finding a new way forward is an old tradition.

Phyllis Tickle is a woman of strong faith and sharp intellect. She served as religion editor for *Publishers Weekly* for many years and is deeply committed to her local church. In her excellent and comprehensive work *The Great Emergence: How Christianity Is Changing and Why*, Tickle dives deep into the consideration of the historical context for change in the church and in our culture's relationship to the church. Changes in the world and in culture do not alter the nature of God, but as history shows us, they do alter the shape of the church and the way faith is practiced. Political, economic, technological, and social changes all weave together to shape our world. Tickle postulates powerfully (and backed by credible research) that the changes we are navigating at this time in history are nothing short of the entrance into a new chapter in Christendom.

I would like to suggest that when we look through the broader lens of the historical context at the growing number of non-goers, we may find, as did Jamieson, that these are not isolated, rebellious Christians, but that in fact, non-goers may be part of something new that God is up to in the world. As we make an effort to understand the times we have been given to live in, we are better able, as were the people of Issachar, to have a sense of how to be a part of what God is doing.

Taking Flight

The Spirit is moving, and many non-going Christians are finding meaningful ways to have a full and healthy spiritual life. It is undeniable that the visible and established structures of the institutional church hold a time-honored place for rituals that mark important crossroads: confirmation, baptism, weddings, funerals, common liturgy, the thread of history, and keeping of theology. The structure, funding, and resources of the church offer unique support to our kids as they grow up and to all of us as we seek to understand theology and organize ourselves to make a difference in the world. With this in mind it is wise to ask what new questions and gaps this Wild Goose shift may raise.

My friend Teresa, a gifted musician, artist, and also a non-goer for some years, asked me as I wrote this book, "What will I tell my grandchildren?" I have other friends who hear the cry of the Goose but linger in their church congregations because of these questions. Pastors and priests are fair to raise these concerns for those who leave. These are not questions of skeptics but of earnest inquiry. They must be asked. Even in my own community and the communities of those I mentor, these questions present themselves. To be sure, especially when it comes to children and teens, it takes work and intention to nurture healthy spiritual and social development. A collective narrative is important for all of us but is especially important for children and youth and for adults in the early stages of spiritual or personal formation. What will it look like for our non-goer communities to gather around our children and raise them up in love and faith? In many ways, the art of non-going and facilitating alternative Christian communities that offer the support we might need, is still in the works.

Echoing this challenge and opportunity, Linda, a friend who is a newer non-goer, remarked on her experience thus far: "Dividing the truth of God from church activity can be a courageous, anxiety-filled adventure." I agree with Linda. It will take intention, effort, and care to carry new generations into the future well and to maintain a strong and faithful strand of the Christ story into the world as non-goers. It can be a scary adventure. I do at times worry about that responsibility as a community leader and as I consider my own children and grandchildren. It comforts me to remember this: when the first Jesus followers threw down their nets, they had no idea what they were getting into. When the Protestant Reformers parted ways with the Roman Catholic Church, they didn't have new forms in place to replace the structures that had shaped their way of life. When Francis of Assisi flung his father's fortunes in the street and set out to form a new community of faith, he had no idea what would be born. Charting a new course does mean there will be uncertainty.

Although there is much to be learned along the way, a thoughtful consideration and a look about to see what is already springing up is in order. I have now traveled some years and some distance following the cry of the Wild Goose. Although the way may not be tidy and contained, from what I have seen so far, if you hear the call, the journey is worth taking.

◈ Questions and Action ◈

1. Leonard Sweet recognizes a hunger for community and for being part of something today. He calls this EPIC (Experience, Participation, Image-Driven, and Connection—or more simply, doing, joining in, seeing, and connecting). Do you in any way recognize this shift toward EPIC in your own life or in the lives of others around you?
2. What does the phrase "spiritual but not religious" mean to you?
3. What in this chapter stirs the most uncertainty or discomfort for you?
4. What in this chapter stirs the most hope for you?

FACE-TO-FACE

Companions for the Journey

The structure of church often provides a variety of opportunities to touch the lives of others and to form healthy relationships. Without the structure of church, how can we proceed? How can the life of non-goers be built around cultivating relationships and caring about people? What can happen when we slow down and tune in enough to share ordinary gifts and ordinary time?

This chapter explores what can take place when we open ourselves to the possibilities around us every day. When as non-goers we reach out, we can carry the presence of Christ with us. With that in mind, let the following stories help to reassure you that without church, there are still many ways to offer blessings, extend hospitality, find mentors and mentees, share your gifts, and learn from others.

The Portable Blessing—Passing the Peace

Everywhere I turned, someone approached with a warm embrace or a hand outstretched in welcome. There were no pseudo-polite greetings—no "I love your handbag!" or "Can you believe this rain?" or even "Cool tattoo, dude." The absence of chatty exchange was a relief to an introvert. Instead, echoing around the room, I heard "Peace be with you," followed by the warm reply, "And also with you." Men, women, and children moved from person to person, making certain that everyone had been touched and had received the blessing of peace. A wizened old lady spoke with vigor as she reached for my shoulder. A beefy man in a flannel shirt and blue jeans spoke softly as he extended his hand.

This was not a meet and greet. This was the liturgical practice of Passing the Peace—an act of worship, a recognition that we each carry Christ with us. I felt a little awkward joining in this unfamiliar exchange, but at the same time I felt pleased and very included in my first experience of this celebration of the presence of Jesus. I was raised in churches where we mostly sat looking at the backs of heads. While I might have a good idea how rapidly someone's hair was thinning, in most cases I was not invited to look into the eyes of the person with thinning hair in a way that would remind us both that Christ was present. Although this initial experience was some years ago now, the practice of Passing the Peace never fails to move me.

"Peace be with you." These were the first words Jesus spoke to his disciples after his resurrection. No matter what our circumstances are or what craziness is going on in the world, we can remind each other that Christ is present—the peace of Christ is with us. We are not alone. A simple kindness, eye contact, and human touch bring a blessing wherever we are. With church attendance on the decline, plenty of churches where we are more acquainted with hairlines than with eyes, and lifestyles that isolate us from people, how can we pass the peace and impart the presence of Jesus to others?

By simply taking the time to behold those we encounter throughout our day, we can pass on the peace of Christ. Jesus was amazing at beholding. He stopped and noticed people who might not have been noticed. He looked at them—I mean really looked at them—gazing into their faces and their eyes, a rare gift. And often when he did so, healing occurred. Jesus noticed Zacchaeus the tax collector perched in a tree and called him down to dinner and to a whole new life. In Luke 13 Jesus noticed a woman who had gone unnoticed for eighteen years, bent over by illness and out of direct line of sight. He saw her, reached out, touched her, and she was healed.

Our days are filled with moments to behold one another. We can take the time to simply slow down and notice our kids or family members without any agenda. We can turn to our literal neighbors and go out of our way to greet them and take time to listen to them. Sharing our time, our stories, our garden bounty extends peace. We can even pass the peace to complete strangers.

Try this: Next time you go through a grocery checkout aisle, a fast-food drive-through, or up to a banking window, pause before you make your transaction. Make a point to establish eye contact with the person who is helping you. Smile and continue to hold eye contact while you ask with sincerity, "What has this day been like for you?" Then be quiet and wait in anticipation of a response. Invariably, you will get a quick look of surprise, followed by a light in the other person's eyes. You aren't averting your gaze or chatting on the cell phone while they serve you like the last person who came through their line did. You are taking time to actually see them—a person, not a commodity or a vending machine. Think of it as a spiritual practice, the practice of beholding others.

Sometimes the reply to your question will be the customary, "Just fine." Other times a sincere inquiry makes way for a sincere answer: "My baby is sick and I didn't sleep at all last night." Or, "Wonderful! I just got engaged!" No matter the reply, in that few seconds of interaction a human connection is made, and you are both the better for it. Small gifts of time and attention can change a day. We all know it. In this culture, time and attention are two of the most valuable gifts to give. We are all hungry for these ourselves, but we can tend to have a short supply for others.

I have been paying attention to my own behavior this week while writing this chapter. It has been a long week with many demands on my time and my emotional energy. Consequently, I have been making more runs through drive-up windows for banking, coffee, dry cleaning, and food-on-the-go than I care to admit. I've dashed in and out the door with a quick hello to my son or husband without really stopping to listen to them. I am embarrassed to say that this week my first inclination has been to avoid eye contact and not expend any extra energy with anyone—just get on by with minimal output. Sometimes this is just what I have done.

Other times, however, I have caught myself in the act of avoidance in time to stop short and open myself up long enough to look right in the eye of another person—another passenger on the bus, someone who is serving me, my kids, or the elderly neighbor lady who likes to chat—so that I really see them and really engage in a moment of human connection. I always end up feeling better for it, and I can tell the person on the other end has felt seen as a person and better for it too. But for this introvert, it takes extra effort. I think it might be worth saying again: We are all hungry for time and attention. These are two of the most valuable and healing gifts we can give.

In his thought-provoking and practical book *a.k.a. Lost*, my friend Jim Henderson calls this practice "paying attention." Many people will never step through the door of a church, and even if they do, they may not receive a blessing. Many people go through the day without a kind word spoken to them or real eye contact made with them. When we pay attention, we pay the highest compliment. Every day we carry Christ wherever we go; we carry the presence of Christ along, a portable blessing. What would the world look like if we, the "church scattered," went about our days paying attention, practicing truly beholding others and passing the peace in natural ways?

I don't know about your town, but in the Portland metro area it is not uncommon to encounter sign-holding women or men at traffic intersections, sometimes even with their children or their pets alongside. A number of years ago, when my children were little, I began to wrestle with this situation. What did I want my kids to learn from these drive-by encounters? Who did I want to be in these moments? How did my desire to follow Jesus inform me as I pulled up to the intersection? What I did know was that when I intentionally ignored the person standing there I felt cold and less than human. I tried the smiling strategy. Now I felt fake and insulated—warm and well fed in my cozy car, I could wave and drive away, disregarding their request. A few times I tried sticking a five-dollar bill out the window to see how that felt. Not so good either—I felt uneasy for assuaging my guilt in a way that might be causing harm.

I wanted my kids to have a sense of how to relate to need and to other human beings, and I wanted to have less inner turmoil in these intersection dilemmas. My friends in social services assured me that giving money was not generally the most helpful response. Here is a solution I came up with: I found some nifty tuna salad and cracker snack packs at the wholesale grocery. I bought cases of them and kept the door pocket of my minivan filled with them at all times. When I would approach an intersection with a sign-holding person, I was ready. At first I wondered if the tuna packets might be greeted with disdain. This was a tiny snack, not money, not a meal. I was surprised to find that the tuna and the friendly stop to say hello was consistently warmly received. Sometimes the packet would be torn into on the spot and other times tucked into a backpack for later. I am pretty sure the warm response was not about the nifty tuna pack. I think the act of stopping and engaging is what mattered.

My kids got excited about keeping an eye out for anyone who might need a package of what had become known as "Seed Tuna" (so named because it helped seed good things in the world; others picked up on the idea and began to practice seeding goodness at intersections too). "Mom! Go that way! There is someone we can give Seed Tuna to." At times they spotted someone across the freeway and clamored for me to change my course and make sure we got to meet the person on the other side of the road. Now instead of calculating avoidance techniques we were going out of our way to meet a new person. Instead of feeling disconnected and awkward (separated by our car and our privilege) we recognized how connected we were. And as we integrated and connected we did in fact meet Jesus in the hands and faces of the poor.

Of course I talked with my kids about the complexities of these street-corner transactions; about the variety of reasons people might be standing with their signs and the fact that one package of tuna didn't fix everything. We talked about how sharing a tuna snack did not relieve us from responsibility for learning about and working on the systems and structures that cause poverty. We also talked about how it feels when someone takes time to stop and really see us, and how as people who choose to follow Jesus, we, too, can learn to follow his example and stop to really see people.

There is often a large basket of Seed Tuna inside the front door of my house, making it easy to remember to take a refill when I head to my car. And when someone asks why I have a basket of tuna at the door—well, I hand them an armload, tell them our story, and send them off to seed goodness too. No matter who is sitting at that intersection and why they are there, they are fellow human beings, made in the image of God. We can pass the peace and carry the presence of Jesus as we stop to see each other this way. Remember, passing the peace is not some newfangled idea I cooked up or the next seeker-friendly tool for our evangelistic toolbox. It is a practice from the deep well of Christian tradition, sparked by the words of Christ and carried on for centuries.

With Doors Wide Open—Practicing Radical Hospitality

In Romans 15:5–7 Paul gives these instructions to followers of Jesus: "May the God of endurance and encouragement grant you to live in such harmony with one another, in accord with Christ Jesus, that together you may with one voice glorify the God and Father of our Lord Jesus Christ. Therefore welcome one another as Christ has welcomed you."[1] And how does Christ welcome us? With absolutely no reservations. With arms wide open. With love that sees us in all our brokenness and all our beauty (both are resident in each of us) and always takes us in.

Dorothy Day is one of my great heroes in the faith. Day was a determined and intelligent woman with her heart wide open in response to the teaching of Jesus and to the poor, whom Jesus so freely welcomes. Drawn by Christ's message of radical hospitality and welcome, she came to Jesus in the middle of the Great Depression and a world at war. Day was a passionate young leftist intellectual when she met Peter Maurin, a devoted Roman Catholic with a determination to "live in accordance with the justice and charity of Jesus Christ."[2] She found the Jesus she learned about through Maurin's explanation of Catholic social teaching to be compelling. Catholic social teaching includes a strong sense of the dignity of every person, paired with Communitarianism, which, put simply, is the belief that people are shaped in the context of community and we must balance individual rights with the best interest of the whole community in mind. For Dorothy Day, that understanding of Jesus translated into hands-on action and a passionate faith and devotion to Jesus.

In 1934, Day dove into life in a New York City slum. She started by founding the *Catholic Worker* newspaper to help spread the idea that social justice and faith belong hand in hand and demand a peaceful reconstruction of the social order. The newspaper headquarters, also home for Day and her young daughter, soon became known as a "house of hospitality." As the message of the *Catholic Worker* hit the streets, people in need began to knock on her door. She, along with her newspaper staff, welcomed strangers in to share a hot meal and have a safe, dry place to sleep. In a short time the Catholic Worker movement became known for truly being hospitable to all people, especially to people on the margins of society.

Day believed strongly in weaving together the practical and the spiritual. Prayer and study were in complete harmony with making up beds on the floor and stirring large pots of soup, and these were all in harmony with producing a lively newspaper that provided an alternative Christian perspective in a time of war and hunger. While Day was inspired by Roman Catholic teaching, her work was conducted outside church. She integrated her beliefs into her life, making her a true example of how to be a Christian without going to church.

The importance of valuing all people, practicing economic justice, being good stewards of creation, promoting peace, making a place for each person to participate in the life of the community, and standing in global solidarity were all strong principles that marked her community. These principles were not plucked out of the pool of politically correct rhetoric. They were and are born of a theology that has been described as believing "that the true foundation of hospitality is the mystical body of Christ—the original unity of all persons that can be made visible and restored by the redeeming works of Christ"[3] as put into action by Christ's followers. Within only five years, this theology and understanding of Jesus brought the newspaper a circulation of 190,000 and birthed thirty new Houses of Hospitality. Today there are at least two hundred Houses of Hospitality located around the world. Although they were inspired by the Catholic Worker model, not all are Catholic. They are, however, committed to the same principles and the welcome of Christ that motivated Dorothy Day.

Hospitality is a lot of work, but for me it brings a great deal of joy. My practices are a far cry from those of Dorothy Day, who went further than most of us ever will with true hospitality. Some people come more naturally to hospitality, but it is a Christian discipline for all of us to engage. I probably came to my disposition toward an open door through my Grandma Irene, wife of rural pastor Grandpa Wilmer Briggs. They lived simply, but she always found enough food to serve an extra person, enough clothing in her closet to share, and a warm welcome for anyone passing through. My dad followed his mother's example and frequently, without advance notice to us, he would invite people over for meals or bring home hitchhikers to sleep on the couch (a practice to be approached with more caution these days to be sure, but it made a positive impression on me).

It should be noted that Ken has been one to share what we have and open our home with ease too. Without our common vision, our life would be different. Since we married thirty-one years ago, more than thirty-four people have lived with our family. (I think we've lost count now.) We started with a pregnant teen, then a woman and her two children who had been living out of their car; and at various times my younger teenage and college-age sisters moved in. We were home base for missionaries on furlough, a bridge home for friends in financial crisis, a safety net for a young couple and their baby who were having a hard time making ends meet, and for a young divorcée and her toddler son as she worked to get on her feet after leaving an abusive relationship. We shared our home with friends who had three young children while they built a house, made a place for Japanese exchange students, took in a high school friend of our daughter's as her parents went through a painful divorce, and enjoyed the companionship of a friend who sold all he had in preparation to travel the world in search of what was next. Some of these thirty-four-plus we knew well, some we didn't know at all, and some we knew only casually or through someone else.

For years our home has been an open house. Literally. We seldom lock the doors, and friends come and go with a tap on the door. I have fed more teens than I can count and counseled even more weary souls over a cup of tea. I share my books and tuck tired college students in on the couch for a therapeutic nap. In the process, I have been filled up and stretched to grow in new ways. Now mind you, there are drawbacks: stained carpet, little children running unsupervised and falling into my care by default, the difficulty of carving out time for Ken and me in our own home without other people around, listening to other people quarrel, having other people hear us quarrel, hearing other people's babies scream in the middle of the night, cross-cultural misunderstandings, more messes to clean, and more life stories to carry. But the truth is that I don't regret a bit of it.

With each new household member we learn, through trial and error, more about how to make our expectations clear, how to set boundaries, how important it is to share the load of day-to-day household maintenance, how to plan time for ourselves and our family, how to live with all sorts of personality types, how to say no, and how important it is to play together and not let life get too serious. My husband has the helpful combination of a huge heart and an ability to retreat to our bedroom for solace when he needs space. When we had people living with us, we made an extra effort to set aside time for our family and for each of our children. They knew they were our priority and that if they had something to say about the open house they could speak and be heard. They learned to share and be flexible, and in their younger years they enjoyed the attention and variety of new friends young and old.

It is fair to note that in most of these years, we had the advantage of owning a home that had extra space, a budget that could stretch to feed extra people, and the luxury of flexible schedules. While these are matters of privilege, I can tell you that some of the most hospitable people I have been blessed to know live on meager incomes and sometimes don't know how they will make it from month to month. When we share what we have—whatever that may be—hospitality can make a difference.

The role of being surrounded by supportive community comes into play here too. On many occasions our open home was supported by the broader body of Christ. Friends showed up to help with deep cleaning to prepare for new household members. When extra beds and bedding were required, the word went out and sure enough, beds and bedding appeared. A side of beef was gifted at a time when we were preparing dinner for over a dozen people daily. When we needed a break, kind people provided babysitting or a beach cabin getaway. We were not in it alone, and that made all the difference.

When we, the community of Christ, examine the scriptural call toward hospitality together and then we work together, we can stretch our imaginations and our comfort zones. It is important to keep in mind that sometimes we need to first be hospitable to ourselves, close that open door, and focus inward for a season. When it is time to open the door, when we welcome the wayfarer, the immigrant, the homeless, the displaced, the lonely, the single parent, we incarnate the welcome of Jesus and we ourselves are transformed.

We have been on the receiving end too—the recipients of hospitality that has brought renewal and refreshment. Three couples dear to us, the Ares, the Brunkens, and the GGs, come to mind as refuges of hospitality for us for many years, opening their homes and making time for us at points that our house and our life were feeling a little too full and we really needed a respite. With a gracious welcome, finely prepared food and drink, peaceful surroundings, a willingness to take hours to listen to all the stories of life, and an understanding that we weren't likely to return the favor anytime soon, we have been held steady by their gifts of hospitality and welcome.

You may not want thirty people to live with you, and that's okay; just don't underestimate the difference a simple evening of friendship and kindness can make to carry someone forward. And I am speaking from experience. Don't sell short the power of a bowl of homemade soup with crusty bread, a bottle of wine, and a listening ear. Chances are, you can offer that.

Light from the Mentoring Constellation

Let me tell you more about my non-goer friend Arnie. He pretty much rocks when it comes to beholding people and sticking with it for the long haul. Arnie is an artist, entrepreneur, and metal fabricator in the early stages of retirement. And as I told you earlier, although he and his wife, Sharon, served congregations as active lay leaders for many years, Arnie is, and has been for some time now, one of the growing number of Christians who no longer find their place in the institutional church. Still, his faith runs deep, he has an insatiable thirst for learning, the study of Scripture, church history, and theology. Interestingly, he often finds himself serving as a confidante and mentor for leaders who remain in the church.

Arnie was formed through plenty of life experience, soul-searching, and personal work. He learned a lot the hard way as a wild young man before an encounter with Christ that changed his direction. As an older leader in the church, he was forced to face his own demons when he fell into an extramarital relationship. He chose to confront his failing and to work along with Sharon to rebuild their marriage together. He suffered the terrible loss of a beloved son in an automobile accident. Through it all he determined that he'd keep growing and learning and helping others if he could.

As a small business owner, Arnie has had his own shop for many years. One of his enterprises and artistic hobbies is designing and building custom cars. His craftsmanship and creativity have captured the attention of many, including the staff of well-known car magazines. His open-shop policy and the inspiration of his work began to make the shop a favorite destination for men (and an occasional woman) to gather and work on their own projects. Arnie would work alongside those people, asking good questions and giving them his full attention. Invariably, over time they would open up and share their darkest struggles and most difficult challenges and discover they were accepted. I have observed Arnie do this for years. He didn't think of his role as anything special. He was just being himself, following his passion for building cars and putting his hard-won life experience to good use.

About nine years ago, a young man, recently released from serving jail time, was working for Arnie. He experienced the same sort of good questions and the deep gift of attention as the other guys who'd come to the shop for years. He told Arnie that he thought of him as a mentor and asked Arnie if he would meet with him formally to help him with practical steps as he rebuilt his life. Arnie said yes. That experience opened Arnie's eyes to see himself more clearly. He'd lived some life, faced his own darkness, experienced redemption, and done the hard work to continue moving forward. He had something to offer.

Arnie doesn't advertise himself as "mentor." He shrugs his shoulders and tells me that he simply makes himself available to people who show an interest in personal growth. He now spends up to several hours a day meeting with men and women who are pursuing that growth. "It always starts with a good conversation," he explained in a quiet voice. "After that conversation, I might offer to meet for coffee. Then it is up to them. Not infrequently they will end up asking if we can do this regularly." He recently helped a young entrepreneur build her own successful new business, he meets weekly with a young man who leads an influential citywide ministry, and he walks with men struggling with addiction and financial disarray. He collaborates with and cheers on a young ceramics artist as she practices her art and builds her business. In many cases he sees himself as part of a holistic support team. For example, someone he meets with might also have a therapist and an AA sponsor.

Arnie said about two-thirds of his mentees choose to think of their relationship as a mentoring relationship, and about one-third think of it as just a weekly coffee meeting with a friend. It doesn't matter to him what he is called—friend or mentor. But if he and a mentee are working on, for instance, establishing wise business practices, you can bet they are also talking about the emotional health of the person. If they are working on a broken relationship, they will likely also take a peek at financial and physical health. His holistic approach to relationship is deeply rooted in his own faith. Not all the people Arnie meets with identify as being Christian, but most find themselves curious about Arnie's faith. Often, the changes that take place over time involve a deepening or new commitment to God.

"This is a commitment for as long as it takes," Arnie said. "I don't mind if people need to take baby steps, but some action is needed to keep going forward. Some people want to be heard but are not interested in change. If they want to change, I am there. Maybe it will take six or eight years—that's okay. This is real life, not a program. It is about discovering and learning to appreciate and value this person's life and experience. The style is conversational rather than systematic; we don't read books and answer specific questions. We look at their story and ask what is working and what isn't. When something isn't working, then I can help them look a little deeper and become more aware. It is about asking good questions for them to answer for themselves."

I asked him who mentors him. He told me about a valued friend who is a psychologist and a peer who offers him good advice and counsel. "My close friendships that are based on mutual appreciation and common interest are essential."

Another essential ingredient is that Arnie knows himself and is well aware that he certainly isn't a saint. His honesty about himself prevents the guru syndrome and inspires people to realize that they, too, can begin to reach out to others and make a difference. "Don't wait till you feel you have it all together to help others. There is always someone to give a hand up. There is a way to bring your own experience to help someone else."[4]

About a decade ago, I was leading with very few supportive networks and even fewer role models. That all changed for me after I participated in a workshop designed to help clarify where and how God was working in my life. One segment of the workshop was focused on mentoring. Up to this point, I'd never had a formal mentor, never considered myself a mentor, and honestly had never thought all that much about mentoring. My image of a mentor was an old person with boundless wisdom. If a person was lucky enough to be noticed by such a mentor, they would be taken under their wing and instructed in all manners of life, sort of guru/master like. Quite frankly, I probably wouldn't have been interested in giving any one person this much authority in my life.

Paul, the presenter of the workshop, shook up this concept of mentoring for me. He was using a mentoring discovery process developed by Terry Walling. First of all, he shattered the notion that a mentor needs to be older, all-knowing, and practically perfect. In fact, he suggested you could be mentored by a number of people at once, someone for one particular purpose—gardening, for example—and someone else for another purpose—like centering prayer. The gardening person might not be someone you would want to seek out for mentoring on marriage, but they might grow a mean zucchini. When we realize that finding a mentor doesn't mean finding "The One Person" who can help us in all areas of our life, the possibilities open wide. The expanded concept of mentor means that we are all surrounded by many potential mentors.

As a non-goer, it can take some extra intention to maintain healthy, well-balanced support systems and opportunities to share our gifts with others. I have discovered constructing and then cultivating a mentoring constellation to be a very helpful practical tool in my growth as an individual and in community life. This same workshop included a paradigm-shattering exercise that guided the participants in creating a full mentoring constellation rather than a model dependent on the fantasy of finding a lone guru. The constellation is made up of a balance of people on the vertical axis who could be mentors to you and mentored by you.

For me, this mentoring constellation tool, when taken seriously, is a means to personal formation and to forming others, ultimately empowering and releasing. In the words of Brian McLaren this is "disciple-formation and disciple deployment," equipping people to meet the needs of a world looking for connection and meaning. This tool for intentionally seeking growth and sharing with others has served as a "disciple-formation and disciple-deployment" tool in my life.

Here is my own rendition of the process that honestly changed my paradigm and, literally, my life.[5] If you'd like to give this exercise a try, here's what you need: sticky notes approximately one inch in size and, if possible, in five different colors; a Sharpie pen; and one large piece of paper. I suggest the paper be at least 14 x 22 inches, and taping four pieces of plain paper together works great.

This exercise can be done on your own, but even better, find others to try this out with you and share what you discover when you complete the exercise.

Get ready to brainstorm.

Step 1: Briefly review your life, thinking of all the people who have influenced you in a positive way and helped you to become who you are today: family members, teachers, neighbors, coaches—anyone who comes to mind. Start at an early age and work forward. Choose one color of sticky note to use for this. As names come to you, write down each name on its own sticky note. As I did this, I remembered my fifth-grade teacher, Mrs. Sherman, who helped me struggle through my multiplication tables and learn to love poetry and van Gogh. I thought of Leo, a youth group leader who had more confidence in me than I did in myself as a young person, and of Karen, a college roommate who exposed me to Christian social justice by sending me a subscription to a progressive Christian magazine. I was shocked to discover I had dozens of names to add to notes. These are "Direct Mentors."

Step 2: Now think of other significant influences. It could be that the words or works of a particular author, blogger, poet, or artist have made a significant mark on you. You probably do not know these people personally, but they count too. Choose a second color of sticky note and, again, write each name down on its own note. Author Madeleine L'Engle, my friend Jen Lemen and her inspiring work, National Public Radio (NPR), and the writings of Henri Nouwen came to mind for me. These are called "Indirect Mentors."

Step 3: Now think of the friends in your life currently with whom you can share on a deep level and who do the same with you. Write their names down on their own sticky notes, using yet another sticky note color. A veritable wealth of names tumbled out for me: Molly, Sharon, Marcie, Ken, Karen, Christine, Deb, Jim, Gayle, Tamara, Lori, Michelle; my sisters Kim, Adele, and Kari; my mom . . . These are "Horizontal Mentors."

Step 4: Next think of people in your life to whom you already offer, or might begin to offer, something of your experience, and write their names down on notes of another color. Just a few names came to my mind, and I realized that my constellation was going to be a little top-heavy. These represent "Downward Mentoring."

Step 5: Last, consider what you might like to be mentored in. Write each category on its own note. Don't worry about who will do the mentoring. Do break these down into specific items; for example, I wrote prayer, personal budgeting, Myers-Briggs Type Indicator, preaching, and organizational skills.

You may be surprised by how many notes you have made. Now you will need the large piece of paper and your Sharpie to organize them. Placing your paper horizontally, draw a large X in the center of the paper going from corner to corner. Then add a horizontal and vertical axis with arrows (see the diagram on page 90). Write your name in the center. In the top section write "Upward," and in the bottom section write "Downward." On the left side of the X write "Inside Horizontal," and on the right side of the X write "Outside Horizontal." Now in the top section add the words "Direct" to the left of "Upward" and write "Indirect" to the right of "Upward."

Now for those sticky notes.

First you'll work with the top section. Notice that the Upward quadrant is split into two halves: Direct and Indirect. Start by placing the notes from Step 1 (the direct mentors) in the Direct half. Then put the notes from Step 2 (the indirect mentors) in the Indirect half. Review the Direct names. Look for any people who may be presently mentoring you and add a star on those notes.

Next you'll work with the left and right quadrants, labeled Inside Horizontal and Outside Horizontal. Read through the names from Step 3. Some of these people may be part of your day-to-day life (work, home, spiritual community, other). Place those notes in the Inside Horizontal section. Other notes from Step 3 may be people you see less and with whom you don't frequently share a common context but who offer valuable perspective. Put their names in the Outside Horizontal section.

Move on to the notes from Step 4, which list people to whom you already do or might begin to offer something. Place those names in the Downward section.

Mentoring Constellation

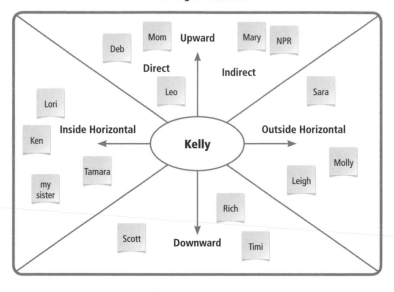

For the sake of space, this sample diagram shows only a few of the people who were named on my sticky notes and ended up part of my constellation.

Review your constellation. Is there something missing? Do you have one section more heavily weighted than another?

What do you see on the vertical line? Are you mostly giving to others without someone to mentor you? Or perhaps the opposite is true—do you have plenty of opportunity to learn and grow but few people you are helping along? Perhaps at one time you had upward mentors in your life but this exercise reminds you that you currently don't. You can evaluate what may be missing and where you have strong support.

Now check out the horizontal line. Do you have friends who can offer good perspective? Are all these friends immediately involved in your day-to-day life? Or do you also have friends from completely different contexts? If you only have advice from people who are immediately in your life, your perspective will be limited. Also, sometimes it is easy for Christians to realize that they have lost connection with people who don't identify as being Christian. Check that out for yourself too.

Once you have reviewed this constellation, you can refine it and make a plan of action. If you see gaps, consider how they can be filled to bring more balance. I've tried this exercise on friends and family members. They all agreed it was a worthwhile experience and that they'll make use of it. Several suggested that they wanted to refer to their constellation over time to evaluate how they are developing.

What might it look like to take specific action to balance and grow your mentoring constellation? When it comes to finding new mentors, here are some considerations:

One reason mentoring can sound daunting is that people tend to think of a mentoring relationship as a lifelong commitment—once a mentor, always a mentor. Although our friend Arnie is willing to sign on for six to eight years, that is an unusual level of commitment. It is also common to hope that a potential mentor will be the one to take the first step, noticing a potential mentee and approaching them. Although this may happen sometimes, it isn't usually the case.

Instead of thinking this way, get specific. Think about reasonable time frames. Identify exactly what you'd like to be mentored in and how long it might take to achieve. Once you have done this, take a chance and approach your potential mentor. Tell them what you appreciate about them and what you'd like to be mentored in. Ask if they would be willing to meet with you for a set period of time to help you forward in this particular way. Give them time to think about their answer and the frequency of meetings. For example, "Meg Brown, you are an amazing preacher. I am wondering if you'd be willing to meet with me once a month and exchange email communication twice a month for the next six months, to mentor me in my preaching." When it is broken down like this, Meg, even if she is a very busy or even famous person, might see a way to say yes. Let them know you don't expect an answer at that time and that you understand if this commitment isn't possible for them right now. I have friends who have written favorite authors they've never met to make such a request and have received yes for an answer.

Now return to the notes that hold what you'd like to be mentored in from Step 5. Do you already know people who might be good mentors for those areas? Write their names down on the corresponding sticky note. Are you aware of people you don't personally know yet or don't know well but might like to be mentored by? Don't be hesitant. Write down their names.

After I completed this exercise, I jumped in, both feet first. I started by asking presenter Paul if he would mentor me as a developing leader. He said yes. Over time that initial mentoring relationship shifted to a horizontal mentoring relationship as I became a mentor for Paul. Now, years later, we are friends and ministry partners planting an intentional community together. I have had remarkable women and men mentor me to grow in practicing the presence of God, gaining organizational skills, serving as a pastor, developing as an artist, gaining cross-cultural fluency, and more. With the help of the nifty mentoring constellation tool, I had gone from feeling I had no role models to having a wealth of mentors and supportive resources. Also, over the years, I've become mentor to many others as well.

When it comes to mentoring others, start by looking around you. You have something to offer. Try the Arnie model: Strike up conversation and ask good questions. Who knows what may come of being open, listening well, and being willing to share what you have? Now that I've had the privilege of mentoring a good number of people, I have to admit that I probably learn more than they do as we meet over time—and I love it! And if you think about it, Jesus went a long way with the simple model of mentoring/discipling twelve people, who then went on to reach many others. Can you imagine what would happen if every Christian created a strong mentoring constellation? The good news is that mentoring, sharing your spiritual story and practical experience, can be natural and doable. Jesus shared in normal ways. He walked, ate, and chatted with people. He used ordinary illustrations from real life to help people see something new.

What if we all began to recognize that we have something to offer others and that the relational encounters could actually be natural and doable for us as well? What if we were continually aware that we have areas to grow in ourselves and we developed a habit of seeking help for growth? This moves us out of the pew and into the world. When we move out into the world willing to learn and meet others where they are, we change, and others may too. Offering Christ-centered hospitality opens the door to view a way of life that is defined by sharing our true selves, opening our homes freely, beholding others, seeding goodness, and being willing to give our time to notice, listen, and learn. It might mean reaching out the car window to touch another human being, passing the peace as we go through our day, sitting down with someone over a hot cup of tea or a cold microbrew, or leaning over the hood of a car for honest conversation. Relational expressions of community can be healing and life-giving to us and to others. The apostle Paul reminds us to welcome one another as Christ welcomed us—not as an occasional impulse but as a continual practice.

With intention and with action, and even without the structure of the church, we can indeed bring blessings to the world and extend transformative hospitality to others. When we take the initiative to be present to people, to share our gifts, and to always keep learning from others, we extend the light of kindness and the Good News of Christ right where we are to whomever we are with.

❯ Questions and Action ❮

1. This week, try beholding others. Practice paying attention. What do you notice about yourself? What do you notice about the people you behold?

2. Think of a time when you have been especially blessed by an act of hospitality. What made that experience memorable and meaningful to you?

3. What kind of mentor would be a blessing to you right now?

4. What skills or experiences do you have to offer others who are seeking a mentor?

5. Find three other people and some sticky notes and complete the mentoring constellation exercise. Then encourage each of them to find three other people and lead them through the exercise, and then they can find three people . . .

GOD WITH US

Art, Music, and the Creative Process

Without Sunday morning service, Sunday night church pot-luck, and Tuesday night choir practice, how can non-goers meet up and what can they invite their friends and neighbors to join them for?

Some people attend church so they can be part of the worship team, others love serving on the Altar Guild or being part of the group that decorates the sanctuary at Christmas. What might fill the need for these creative connections for non-goers and at the same time provide an opportunity to invite others in? This chapter explores the territory of meeting God and creating community through the creative process and communal effort. Creating can be one way to connect with and worship God, and it's a great way to cultivate relationships. Whether the "making" is music, art, or food, the process of creating something brings people together like nothing else can.

Napkin Rings

There we were, all gathered around a table in a pottery studio with wet clay up to our elbows and small children dribbling ceramic glaze on the floor. Most of us didn't know what we were doing, but by golly we were all in, and we were in together. Our Urban Abbey intentional community was making the "big shift" from using paper napkins to using cloth napkins for our common meals, and we needed napkin rings to identify personal napkins. Resident artist Tamara proposed a community ceramics art night to craft napkin rings and, while we were at it, make ceramic plant markers for our growing neighborhood garden.

As we rolled clay, laughed at our clumsy attempts to embellish the pieces we were making, and encouraged each other to keep at it, we were deepening our connection together. We were a community of Jesus, forming with hopes of seeding good in the world together—even if that good started with something as simple as reducing use of paper products and growing fresh veggies for our neighbors. In our common purpose and in the passion behind our playful evening, we were keenly aware of Christ with us.

Creative Process

What do paint, clay, jam sessions, welding, garden dirt, good recipes, poetry, hand drums, and sidewalk chalk have in common? Each of these can be excellent tools for non-goers to build community. I have had the great joy of being part of a number of communities formed around creative action and what happens when people join together to create. As these communities form, I often sense the presence of Jesus. When we as humans engage in creative action, we embody the Spirit of God the Creator, who formed us to bear goodness in this world. Relational connections and new inspiration can be born when art, music, and creative expression draw people together.

Troy Bronsink, artist and author of *Drawn In: A Creative Process for Artists, Activists, and Jesus Followers*, writes, "Artistic creativity uniquely transforms one thing into another.

It introduces novelty to a relationship. It observes things for what else they are."[1] That transformative power means "community can be built through art when it disarms our prejudice, blurs our ideological barriers, and invites us into deeper relationship."[2]

We are all familiar with the image of the solitary artist holed up in their studio, cut off from the world, absorbed in their creative process. For me, that can be a lonely way to create. My best work as a painter (something I don't do nearly enough of these days) has been done in an open studio full of light with other artists working alongside, offering fluid feedback and constructive critique in the middle of the process. I find pleasure in cooking by myself, but nothing beats a kitchen filled with friends chopping, mixing, stirring, and seasoning together. I would never can peaches by myself, but I love a peach canning party complete with a picnic lunch, laughter, and many hands ready for each step of the process. Musician friends attest to the synergy and connection that happens when they sit down to play or sing with other musicians. My little community, Urban Abbey, is building a garden together; my friends at the church Bridge PDX create original music as they write their worship songs together as a community; Shane Claiborne and his community, The Simple Way, together sew their own clothes. Whether creative community takes place in a kitchen, a classroom, an art studio, a public gathering place, or at open mic night at a local pub, there is often no denying that the Spirit is present.

A few months back I had the great pleasure of a chat with iconic but humble-spirited musician and artist Charlie Peacock. Charlie has made his mark in the wide world of musicianship for decades, composing, collaborating, and performing. He works with artists as varied as Ladysmith Black Mambazo, Al Green, Amy Grant, The Civil Wars, and Switchfoot. I have followed Charlie's work for years. I respect his intention to remain connected to "real people in the real world" while retaining his faith. He doesn't isolate himself for long periods of time in Christian culture and Christian circles. In doing so he has had significant influence in many musical spheres, in the lives of both Christians and those who do not identify as Christians. This is what he has to say about creative expression:

> Genuine art making has the effect of broadening community, whereas exclusive art born out of agenda does not. Respecting the gift of art making as a gift from God is the starting place. The church has largely missed this in their urgency to use created things rather than see them as multifunctional—that is, having use and enjoyment. Pleasure is not a dirty word. But it is too often seen as somehow disconnected from the Christian life. Tragic, really. It's a slap in the face of God's creative work. Work that is pleasing is naturally magnetized and so draws people together without slogans, rhetoric, or propaganda. Making is so completely natural to humanity. When we make together we experience our mutual human-ness and calling and so build community, again, without a program. This happens simply by showing up for your making role in the world.[3]

Children are naturals at this. They haven't forgotten their making role in the world. Set out a box of colored chalk on a sidewalk and you have an instant recipe for making new friends and a collaborative art project. Given the opportunity, children can lead the way in community. Their innate curiosity, their sheer joy in "making," and their pleasure in sharing what they have made with others can teach us as we "make" too. When we follow their lead we might find more freedom and pleasure in the process.

It is often over a shared project and natural time together that bonds can be formed and people may grow comfortable enough to share their real stories. The work of lovingly tending a garden with others can become the time when honest prayers are shared. As musicians experiment and make music together, seemingly unlikely relationships can be formed and new possibilities and brilliant ideas are born. God shows up in the meaningful community where shared creative process forms. Charlie Peacock shared this perspective from his own experience.

> Does God show up in the shared creative process? Yes indeed! The ability to improvise music is friendship building and community building. I have gone into a room with people I do not know and made music together, which created the bridge for lasting friendships. I'm thinking of the improvisational recording "Arc of the Circle" I did with saxophonist Jeff Coffin from Dave Matthews Band. More recently I'm thinking of my new friendship with mandolinist Andy Leftwich. It's been this way my whole life, though. I love the mystery of the fruit that comes from an openness to life and surprise. It seldom lets me down. It's as if God keeps saying, "Trust me with the unknown." God will take the unknown and turn it into a known and beautiful thing to see and experience. I prefer to live this way and so I guess I turn my compass toward it more often than not.

Portland ceramic artist Tamara Bryan, tired of working alone in her studio, was motivated to form an artist community comprised of painters, poets, welders, ceramic artists, and graphic designers. I had the good fortune to be part of this group for a couple of years. We gathered in her living room and toured each other's studios and creative workspaces. We shared meals and traded ideas. We engaged in collaborative art projects. We took risks and tried our hand at processes that were new to us. One night we all went to a machine shop to learn to weld together. Another, we collaged as a meditation together. At times we prayed a bit. We told stories of desolation and consolation—times when our inspiration ran dry and times when we were flowing with ideas. We brought each other words of encouragement, and we welcomed Jesus in the middle of it all.

Roving musicians Holly and Ryan Sharp of The Cobalt Season created and experienced Christian community on the road as they traveled around the country performing house concerts for two years. I sat with them at their welcoming kitchen table in Portland, Oregon. We sipped a strong pot of Yirgacheffe as they shared their stories from the road, their two small boys playing at our feet.

As they reflected on those two years, they emphasized the power and importance of temporal, short-term community that can be formed by music. Time and time again they saw community form as small groups of people, sometimes even strangers, gathered to share an evening of music and reflection. Ryan rightly noted that community forms around some sort of common object. In this case, the common object was Christ and the music of The Cobalt Season. They intentionally explored matters of faith and justice while avoiding the use of the language of Western Christian culture.

Holly observed that many smaller Christian communities are decentralized and isolated. Music as a common object can draw these communities together. The shared experience can connect communities and, in the process, it can temper and dispel dysfunction that can come with isolation: arrogance about having found "the right way" to do something, or conversely, nagging self-doubt about charting a new course. A concert in a living room can provide shared experience and lend healthy perspective to overexuberant idealists and offer new space to share wisdom. Interesting one-time or periodic creative gatherings of artists or musicians can create powerful points of connection and Jesus community. Again, in the words of Charlie Peacock, "Lost or not—it's best to travel with friends. So it comes back to community and the joy and struggle of working out our humanity and redemption together in open and closed spaces."

DIY

I occasionally enjoy listening to the PBS radio broadcast *Destination DIY* (Do It Yourself). This show captures a do-it-

yourself culture that my quirky city of Portland character-
izes well. We Portlanders have our own backyard chickens,
make our own pickles, construct our own rain gardens, and
build our own alternative fuel vehicles. Well beyond the funky
culture of Portland, though, it seems that people all over—in
big cities, in suburbs, and in rural areas—are feeling strong
urges to learn how to build their own beds, cobble their own
shoes, bake their own wedding cakes, repair their own plumb-
ing, teach themselves how to play an instrument, and trim
their own trees.

Designer Dmitri Siegel puts it this way: "People don't just
eat food anymore, they present it; they don't look at pictures,
they take them; they don't buy T-Shirts, they sell them."[4] The
Pinterest craze represents this desire to be the creator. Pinterest is a social media tool that allows the user to "pin" images
online on their very own virtual bulletin boards. I haven't
jumped into Pinterest yet, but I've watched my friends' posts
about their Pinterest pursuits. A carefully curated board helps
the user follow through with their own unique DIY projects
and provides a way to easily share ideas and plans with others.

Some of the DIY surge is born of economic sensibility,
some is born out of sheer economic necessity, and some is
born out of a desire for a better world—one that is less about
consumerism and imbued with more personal meaning and
relationship. In July of 2013, NPR's radio broadcast *All Things
Considered* featured food correspondent Allison Aubrey's
story of attending a butter churning party hosted by her neighbors. Even though the butter didn't turn out quite right, the
party was a hit. She told her friend Bee Wilson, British food
writer and author, about the experience. Wilson reflected, "I
think it's kind of a response to the computer age . . . We're
just spending so much of our lives living in a sort-of virtual
capacity, staring at things, that's it very therapeutic to do
things again."[5]

I'm inclined to agree with Wilson, but I'd also add that I
believe this desire to create is in part reflective of a deeper

God-given impulse to create beauty and goodness. Inviting others to participate in the therapeutic creation of beauty and goodness—instead of just staring at things—might be an invitation to a way of abundant life. It interests me that while folks are learning to do these things for and by "themselves," whole communities are forming around the DIY way of life. These communities exist in abundance online, in neighborhood workshops, through community cooperatives, and over backyard fences. It is just more fun, energizing, and reassuring to create together than alone. Communities are creating alternatives that bring a sense of meaning and satisfaction to the uniformity of boxed store products that demand unrelenting consumerism. Rather than making something for themselves, they may even be making something for their neighborhood, community, or a cause they care about. Sometimes what is being made is for a practical purpose, other times it is made for the sheer joy of creating something beautiful and unique. Both are inspired by God's call to us as cocreators.

Making, Baking, and Building

In her book *Down We Go: Living into the Wild Ways of Jesus*, author Kathy Escobar encourages us to think outside the box: "We have to create radically different models of living in community together in a wide variety of contexts. We'll have to turn our attention and energy toward realizing the distinct differences between cultivating communities and building ministries."[6] In my estimation, when considering options for cultivating communities, the temporal community formed by or around music and creativity is not to be dismissed. For non-goers, "making and creating" offer doable, authentic, and refreshing ways to cultivate community. While the form differs from traditional church, the opportunity to deepen friendship and experience the presence of Christ builds communities of possibility. If, as Charlie Peacock said, "Work that is pleasing is naturally magnetized and . . . draws people together without slogans, rhetoric, or propaganda," then being ourselves and pursuing our God-given passions and work with others is a very good place to start building community. Is anyone up for a pickle-making party or a living-room song-writing session? Jesus will be there.

❯❯ Questions and Action ❮❮

1. You may or may not think of yourself as creative, but no matter, you *can* create.
2. Think of something new to try—painting a still life, making jam, planting a herb garden, repairing bikes . . .
3. *Then* (here's the important part) invite at least three other people to join you. Make it into a party and an experiment. Don't take yourselves too seriously; play and give your "making role" in the world a try. See what happens. Then try it again and again.

7

HANDS ON

Cross-Cultural Transformation at Work

Non-goers are rethinking cross-cultural mission and out-reach. They are taking informed action that places relationship at the center. One benefit of being part of a church congregation and structure is the ready-made opportunity to be involved in programs that reach out to folks we might not encounter in our normal day-to-day lives. Mission trips and outreach programs give us an entry point to share resources and learn to see the world from new perspectives. These programs tend to focus on us serving others and trying to meet particular needs.

This chapter captures the stories of non-goers who are seeking to move beyond this more limited approach and reduce the sharp distinction between the sacred and secular. They are fostering genuine friendship and collaboration with "others" and finding ways to participate in God's healing work in the world unrestricted by categories of "us" in the church and "them" beyond our walls.

Friendships on the Street

Ken Loyd leads the way when it comes to field trips to the mean streets of Portland. After a walk down city streets with Ken, it will be clear that you don't need to go far to engage in and learn from cross-cultural relationships. Portland is a hip city with a socially conscious, earth-friendly vibe. It is also a city that has a large youth population on the streets. Ken, a sixtysomething tattooed, pierced, sweetheart of a guy, has spent the last seventeen years of his life building trust and relationships with kids on the streets. He calls it The Underground, a kind of "crazy youth group minus houses." Ken doesn't call these kids "homeless youth"; he calls them "my friends who live outdoors." And when you make friends, you introduce them to your other friends.

For the past three years, in conjunction with Warner Pacific College in Portland, Ken has been introducing friends on the streets to friends on the campus. Andrea Cook, the innovative president of Warner, is leading the small Christian liberal arts college out of an insulated environment as she builds programs that take the urban setting of this school into consideration. With a well-formed urban studies program and holistic Christian ministries program, supportive communal living options for students, and a variety of excellent, down-to-earth internships, Warner is training up young people and leading the way in Kingdom living. Jolynn Davison and faculty member Jess Bielman helped to shape the program, knitting together academics, community, and internships. The Underground is one of the real-life settings where college students will intern during their program.

Senior-year student Nathan Lommasson will tell you without hesitation that his new friendships with people on the streets changed him. Walking the city streets with these friends gave him fresh perspective. He now notices camps he hadn't been aware of under bridges and building demolition that had never registered with him before. He learned that people he'd formerly considered to be without resources know all sorts of amazing things—how to care for pit bulls and train them to be great pets, commit portions of *Hamlet* to memory and recite them, calculate mathematical formulas for piano scales, or play a great game of Frisbee.

What makes these experiences and internships especially formative is that Nathan didn't experience them in isolation. He experienced them in a supportive community with the guidance of a seasoned leader, Ken, and he shared them with the three other students he lived and studied with daily in his Intentional Living house. This is one sterling example of transformative, hands-on discipleship in action. Nathan found a life-giving story and a community of connection with his new friends on the street and with his fellow students as they shared this experience and grew together.

It is important to emphasize that this action is designed to be less about "doing something" and more about forming relationships and allowing those relationships to be vehicles of transformation. If we are motivated by love and begin by building relationships and learning about the cultural and social context we are entering, healthy action that fosters real community will follow naturally.

Nathan plans to be a youth pastor. He assured me that he'd be taking what he learned into his ministry and that it wouldn't all take place within the walls of the church. "I know now that walking on the streets for thirty minutes with a friend who lives outdoors can change someone. I'll be practicing what I've learned at Warner."[1] Nathan has experienced an entirely new model for how to disciple and train up strong leaders and young people with vibrant active faith. What kind of communities could be built and what action would follow if we all took time to walk just thirty minutes with others who have something new to teach us?

Party Hearty

One Sunday afternoon twenty-four years ago, Sharon Darcy and her daughter went on a picnic in a downtown Portland park. They became aware of hungry people sitting nearby, so they shared their sandwiches and chatted with their impromptu picnic guests. The next week Sharon and Shelley decided to picnic again, and this time they invited friends to help them. They all came prepared to open up their picnic table to any who might need food. That Sunday picnic has not stopped since that day. A year later their friend and dedicated volunteer David Utzinger stepped in to carry the tradition forward. Today, up to fifty volunteers from the neighborhood, community groups, churches, synagogues, mosques, high schools, and universities—and up to seven hundred guests—picnic together every Sunday at what's now called Potluck in the Park, rain or shine.

Since that first shared lunch, tens of thousands of people have enjoyed the hospitality of Potluck and have had the opportunity for hands-on experience and friendship building. Volunteers and guests are on a first-name basis and often take time to sit and eat together after the initial lunch rush is done. Over time, everyone gets to know people they might never have spoken with or have come to know otherwise.

In addition to being an event shaped by the spirit of friendship, the beauty of Potluck was and is that it isn't a food line. People have all the choices you might expect to find at a friendly church potluck or a neighborhood block party, and selections vary from week to week. The guests choose what they like and get to enjoy their favorites. Items for vegetarians, special dishes from the Portland Culinary School, fried chicken, fresh salads and fruit, desserts, snacks . . . all the food is provided by volunteers, community groups, churches, and restaurants. In June, when Oregon berries are at their best, a farm just outside the city limits shares huge quantities of delicious red berries with Potluck. Groups of Potluck friends bake hundreds of fresh shortcakes and a nearby hotel whips forty gallons of heavy cream for a tasty local treat and seasonal strawberry Potluck party. A late-summer, old-fashioned barbecue and an annual Christmas Day feast and party knit the Potluck community together and provide opportunities for everyone.

For years my children and I regularly baked pounds of potatoes or boiled dozens of eggs to share at Potluck in the Park. My little red-haired kids would prop themselves up on a milk crate to be at eye level with guests and share food they prepared themselves. We were middle-class folks from the suburbs, and we were fortunate enough to have room in our grocery budget to buy those extra eggs and potatoes, but truth is, we had more to learn than we had to give. I was impacted by the dedication of longtime Potluck volunteer Mary, a wise, slender, soft-spoken recovering alcoholic who'd lost nearly everything before she began to work her recovery program. She gave two full days a week, in contrast to my two days a month, volunteering to keep Potluck going so her neighbors could have a festive meal on Sundays. Every single week Brian, a developmentally disabled young man, made sure that any Potluck guests with wheelchairs, walkers, or crutches had someone to help them as they chose their food.

Cleaning up from the Potluck party is not anyone's favorite job, but the city park needs to be left spotless so we'd all be welcome the next week. Cleanup takes hours and often goes past sundown in the dark winter months. Like a good number of others, Richard was both a regular Potluck guest and a committed volunteer. He was the one who would stay each week until the last pile of recycling was tied with twine and the last pot was loaded into the Potluck van. Richard was brilliant, personable, always ready to lend a hand—and he struggled with mental illness. Richard lived under an overpass and earned money by running a "canning route" in a neighborhood near that overpass. He would go door-to-door, collecting empty cans and bottles and returning them to a store for their five cent redemption value.

One day David Utzinger called to share the sad news that Richard had been struck and killed by a car while crossing the street on his canning route. David wanted to be sure I knew, and asked, "Would you want to join me for the memorial service?" Of course I did. The service was held in a simple chapel in the Southeast Portland neighborhood of Sellwood. There may have been thirty people in attendance. Aside from David, me, several social workers who knew Richard, and one couple who knew him from his canning route, the rest of those in attendance were family members. The family used the time together at the service to speak Richard's story aloud to each other, remember him, lay out the loss and grief they'd experienced on some level for years, remember cherished times together, and honor Richard for who he was.

The sharing was tender and gentle, and the tears flowed freely. I learned that Richard had grown up in a small town with a loving family. In high school he was a star sports player and honors student. Concerns began to arise after Richard went off to university in Portland. Mental illness surfaced and trouble with alcohol followed. He dropped out of university and chose to stay in Portland. Despite the repeated efforts and financial resources of his family, who were willing to provide other options, Richard found he was most at ease when he was living outdoors. Richard had a daily routine of going to the library to complete the *New York Times* crossword puzzle and keep up on the news. He built friendly rapport with the people who lived in the houses on his canning route, and he kept an organized schedule.

A young niece shared that her uncle Richard always remembered her birthday and sent cards. His accomplished twin brother recalled a warm conversation they had at Christmas. A social worker who had a genuine friendship with Richard and stayed in touch with him for years stood to speak poignantly about the effort Richard made to look out for many others on the streets. They all shared about attempts to bring him home or move him indoors, and of their eventual realization that Richard was happiest where he'd chosen to be. Their stories held the history of so much letting go of "the way things should have been" and a great deal of loving acceptance. They told of a man who struggled but who touched the lives of others. They shared their own struggle, but most of all they shared the value of the life of a son, brother, uncle, and friend they loved.

The service wasn't overtly religious, but I felt aware that I was sitting in sacred space as I listened to the family. I, too, began to cry, moved by their unconditional love. While they didn't gloss over the pain in the story, they didn't linger there either. Instead, they shared about the goodness of Richard's life. I felt privileged to have known Richard at least a little bit. Listening to the stories, I wished that I'd known him as more than the most faithful, late clean-up crew friend who slept under the overpass and always had a kind word to say.

At the time of Richard's death, a dear family member of mine was struggling with substance abuse and mental health issues. I was waiting for my loved one to choose to change, and I kept looking for ways to help them "fix their problems." I felt that I couldn't be happy with myself or with them until all was "as it should be." Hearing Richard's family recall the journey they had been on for nearly twenty years gave me some perspective. What if things didn't change? What if the life of my loved one held as much beauty and value right then as the life of Richard, who lived under a bridge and never really sustained recovery? What if my responsibility was to love and not fix? What would that mean for me, and what could my changed posture mean for my loved one? Then I really wept. Because of Richard and his family, after that memorial service I began to slowly find a new way forward in this relationship.

A few months later, in celebration of my birthday, I invited a crew of friends from the suburbs to join me at Potluck in the Park. I asked them, instead of bringing a gift for me, to each prepare a wonderful dish of food for the Potluck and come meet my friends. Most of them had some trepidation about being around homeless people, but because it was my birthday, they came. In the weeks following, a few began to return on their own and bring others along. It all started with a mother and a daughter sharing a sandwich in the park and then inviting friends to bring their sandwiches too. It grew into a weekly Potluck picnic that has changed many. I came to it with the thought that I could help bring a little change in the world by feeding people, but in the end, I was changed the most.

I recommend that non-goers find a way to go outside of their cultural and comfort zone to learn and be changed. Think of something you care about and find a place or a person who can help you navigate that space. When engaging in any kind of cross-cultural setting, it is wise, and I think it is even essential, to find someone who can provide good cultural guidance. David Utzinger and Ken Loyd have helped to orient and educate many people who come to the streets of Portland with good intentions but without an understanding of the complexities of street culture. Many mistakes can be avoided when we are aware that we need good teachers. Any time we enter another culture that is unfamiliar to us, we must remember that our way isn't superior and that there is much for us to learn.

From Party Hearty to Party Hardy

Good guides can teach us from their experience and help us navigate the unfamiliar with less difficulty—we are wise to seek them. Other times our best learning might come as we face personal hardship. I am thankful for the lessons I've learned from others. I am also thankful for what I've learned through personal struggle. At the same time, it's great to know that there are times when learning is a whole lot of fun.

I am fond of creative parties, and in my estimation few things are as fun as a learning party. The New Testament includes chronicles of Jesus party hopping and enjoying people. The fact is, Jesus still does love a good party. And people who would never show up at a church service will show up at a party. Andrew Jones, known as Tall Skinny Kiwi, suggests, "If you want to start a church, just have a party in your house and see who shows up."[2]

The key ingredient for a great party is a host who knows how to connect people and how to create welcoming space. Add good food to share and some storytelling, put on your favorite iTunes playlist, and you're good to go. Andrew is known for saying, "I exist to make friends, give gifts, tell stories, and throw parties!" And he can throw a great one. I joined in a Tall Skinny Kiwi pizza party in Glorieta, New Mexico, a few years back. Everyone had their hands in the pizza dough while Andrew used the creative process to talk about yeast, leaven in pizza, leaven in the Bible, and leaven in our lives. The message stuck. Real experiences go deep.

Non-goers may not want to start a church (as per Andrew Jones's suggestion), but they may find people are naturally drawn together and to the ways of Jesus by parties where stories and goodness are shared. Non-goer friends have hosted wine tastings to raise funds so a friend could travel across the world to help with a medical project, thrown parties to collect a mountain of new socks for people on the streets, created gatherings to make necklaces to be sold for funding of education to help eliminate female genital mutilation, and cooked a simple South African dish together while learning about the history of apartheid.

Jesus thought parties were a good use of his time, and chances are we might find the same to be true. Whether your party is an impromptu pizza-making and storytelling session or a creatively and carefully planned educational, relational, or fund-raising event, there are limitless possibilities for non-goers. Throwing parties can provide opportunity for connection, change, and for relationships to form around meaningful activity and engagement. Let your imagination go!

The Power of Presence

There is great value in learning about others, studying history, educating ourselves about injustice, raising funds for good causes, and caring about global issues. When we take it one step further toward firsthand global experience, we learn on a whole new level. Traditionally, churches and youth groups coordinate short-term mission trips that expose people in their congregation to other parts of their own country or the world. A thoughtfully led trip can help us appropriately share skills and resources with those who have less in the way of material goods than we do. And often, we are changed as we experience the rich cultural and relational resources of others. What kind of travel and "mission" opportunities might make sense for non-goers? As a non-goer who has been notably changed by cross-cultural travel, I have given this question plenty of consideration. I have been leading learning and relationship-building trips to East Africa since late 2007, so I have some personal history and practical experience to draw from here.

"There comes a point in a person's life when you start asking yourself, 'What difference am I making in this world?'"[3] This quote on the home page of Globe Aware, a humanitarian, nonreligious volunteer travel organization, speaks to the growing desire of many people. More and more, Christians, and those who don't identify as Christian, are drawn to make a difference by participating in real experiences rather than just making a financial contribution in response to an advertised need. "Short-term mission trips" were once the domain of enthusiastic youth group members. They are now serious business and, for many people, part of the process of personal development and transformation. Travelocity has joined, in collaboration with the Earthwatch Institute, Cross-Cultural Solutions, Globe Aware, and Take Pride in America, the "Travel for Good" initiative. The Sierra Club offers trips to cut down invasive weeds and learn about other cultures. Generations Touring Company formed a trip to bring travelers to pick up trash in Katrina-affected neighborhoods and make meals for other volunteers after the devastating hurricane; small ad hoc groups of Christians engaged in similar ways. Whether it is hands-on work in the local soup kitchen or hands-on help in a Mexican village, volunteer experiences are drawing people from all stages of life and forming new kinds of community.

I think of two inspiring friends, Leigh Harvey and Diane Ellis, Realtors from Seattle, Washington, who founded Go the Second Mile. For years they used their vacation time to lead quarterly Go the Second Mile service trips to various locations around the world. They are both Christians but often their travelers are not. The travelers are drawn to the stories of team relationships and cross-cultural relationships that are built during these trips and to the meaningful work they can engage in. Second Mile does not evangelize in word, but they do bear good news. In partnership with local leaders in each country, they have built a school in Tibet, helped to start a sewing cooperative in Rwanda, and worked with street kids in Costa Rica and Peru. These efforts are not the efforts of heroes and saviors but of human beings reaching out to learn and to forge friendship.

As well as making a difference for the people they go to serve, trips like these make a difference in the lives of the travelers themselves. Second Mile goes to help, but they also go to learn. Each traveling team meets together prior to taking their trip. Leigh and Diane prepare their travelers to be knowledgeable and respectful of cultural differences, open to learning something new, and aware that our common American assumption—that we know the right way to do things—may not be welcome or may be completely misguided in these cultures.

When teams go with a willingness to be open and learn together, meaningful community is formed and our own perspectives are changed. There is nothing like third-world travel to draw a group together. Lasting friendship and ongoing community often are born out of Second Mile trips. It isn't uncommon for people who leave for one of these trips without a connection to faith to find themselves drawn to the ways of Jesus when they might never have in a church meeting. When Second Mile travelers return home, they stay in touch with each other, work together to raise funds for the people they met overseas, and relate to the world with a new perspective. Long-lasting relationships across the globe and within the traveling communities are forged.

Sometimes travelers have enough money on hand to make trips like these without much financial strain. Other times travelers ask friends and families to support their endeavor and they raise funds to go. Some plan ahead a few years and tuck money away until they have saved what is needed for a trip.

Last year I was introduced to one of the more remarkable women I have ever met. Mary Anne lives with multiple sclerosis and is visually impaired. She is someone who helped me continue to learn that every person has a unique story and has something beautiful to offer the world. I met her when we helped a mutual friend with a move. It was late at night by the time we finished unloading the last box, and Mary Anne needed a ride across town to get home. I offered to make the drive. We were hungry after a hard day's work, and so we stopped at the one place open for food, a Wendy's restaurant. As we ate baked potatoes together, Mary Anne told me some of her story.

Mary Anne lives in a subsidized apartment complex on the transit line in a suburb west of Portland. She gets by on a very modest Social Security Disability check. She doesn't drive and her health doesn't permit her to hold a steady job. Some days she suffers more than others, but she hasn't stopped living a full life. Four years ago she funded her own trip to Uganda, and this year she joined a tour to Israel. She paid for these trips herself by selling discarded items she collected "trash-picking." Taking a sip of her iced tea, Mary Anne stated in a matter-of-fact way, "Yep, I'm a trash-picker."

Using public transit or traveling on foot with a shopping cart to fill, with the limited amount of energy she has for each day, Mary Anne manages to collect and sell enough stuff people have thrown away to pay for these trips. In addition to slowly saving for these big trips, she spends as little as possible each month so that she can keep a savings account and send monthly support for an orphan in Kenya. Mary Anne's story made me realize how easy it is for me to categorize people. If I were to have seen her picking through a dumpster, I am sure I would have felt pity and compassion but would never have imagined who Mary Anne really is and what she brings to the world. Mary Anne's life is not easy, but she has an inspiring, positive spirit and determination, a quick wit, a bright mind, a caring nature, and she isn't afraid to aim for her dreams. After meeting Mary Anne, I am certain that the others on these trips were the better for having had her as a traveling companion.

Mary Anne's "unlikely traveler" story brought to mind Linwood House, a Christian community in British Columbia. Linwood House friends come alongside women who are living on the streets in downtown East Vancouver. Linwood also provides a supportive community for women who are trying to leave the streets. One aspect of this road to a new life involves helping other women. This can include the opportunity for Vancouver women in transition to travel with Linwood House women to Bangkok, where together they volunteer with New Beginnings, a home for Thai women coming out of prostitution. These trips have been redemptive for everyone involved.

It is fair to acknowledge that traveling overseas is generally more accessible to people of a certain class, people with paid vacation time, and people who have the luxury of being able to put money aside for nonessentials. Mary Anne's story may be an exception, and even in her case, in spite of the challenges she does face, Mary Anne has the benefit of a flexible schedule and does not have financial responsibility for anyone else, which frees her more than some. I too was unexpectedly able to make my first trip to Africa in 2007. This trip was only possible for me because of the help of friends. We held events to raise funds, sold stuff, and worked to pull together enough extra money to go to a continent I'd long wanted to visit and learn from. When I was out of the country, friends helped with carpooling and meals for my family. Without a supportive community, it would have been a stretch to be able to go.

I often hear Western friends wrestle with the expense of making such a trip. The internal (or external) quarrel goes like this: "I could spend $4,500 to go on a trip or I could send $4,500 to a reputable organization and feed a lot of children. What is the right thing to do?" The typical inclination is that the best choice is to feed a lot of children. I've thought about this dilemma quite a bit. I am all for feeding children, and I know children who need food. It is a good and fair question to ask. A Kenyan friend, Dr. Edward Simiyu, responds to the question this way: "The power of presence is a greater gift than any money. When you come to be with me, to know me, to learn what my life and my world is like, that makes a difference."[4]

When I think of times when I have faced difficulty in my own life and I remember the people who were willing to step outside of their comfort zone and come be with me, I know he is right. When others are willing to be present to us, it does make a difference. When we are willing to truly be present to others, it changes us. It is also true that when we establish a real friendship and know someone—what their life and world are really like—our motivation for giving and sharing changes. I no longer give to feel good, to change you, or to try to fix a problem. I give because I know and love you. I give with an understanding of your situation and a willingness to learn from you. I give with a better sense of your real need rather than my own idea of what I think is needed. I open myself to learn and receive from you, too, and I become your advocate and storyteller wherever I go. That sort of gift is empowering and transformative all the way around.

All this prompts me to think about what could be possible if non-goers come together and find ways to include others who might not have considered the possibility of cross-cultural travel. Mary Anne's inspiring example and the transformative Linwood friendships in Vancouver and Thailand served as a reminder to me that with ingenuity, patience, and determination to progress slowly, dreams that may seem too big can become possibilities. Cross-cultural engagement, even with a new friend in subsidized housing, can change us. These stories are profound reminders of the power of presence that cannot be measured by dollars and cents. I am intrigued by what small communities of non-goers might do to bring diverse groups of people together for transformative travel—across the world, across town, and in our own hearts.

Global Connections

In 2007 I was one of forty Western leaders invited to participate in the first Amahoro gathering—a leadership conference in Uganda. We forty joined 160 African leaders who came together to explore what an authentic post-colonial African Christian theology, born of African leaders, might look like and how it might empower them to lead their countries and continent forward toward a promising future. The participants from the West were invited as listeners and learners with the intention of building friendships for the long haul. With a wise foundation of preparation, the spirit of teamwork, and encouragement toward listening and humility, the Amahoro demonstrated that it is possible to create transformative community through periodic gatherings. The Amahoro experience changed my life, and the lives of others, in ways that we would never have expected.

Following the conference I opted to travel with several others to Rwanda. Steven Turikunkiko was one of our field trip hosts to this country still in the process of recovering and healing from a horrific genocide. In 1994 nearly one million innocent people were killed in a matter of ninety days, leaving Rwanda in shambles, a country full of traumatized widows and orphans with a deposit of more pain than can be imagined.

It was this pain and need that led Steven and his wife, Providance Uwamariya, despite their own poverty, to take in orphans and assist in the formation of the women's cooperative of genocide survivors. Providance and Steven have more heart, courage, and perseverance than anyone I have ever met. Even though they weren't eating every day, they would never close their door or turn their backs on anyone who sought help. We field-trippers were amazed by what we saw and experienced. A number of us joined together and began to send a small amount of monthly support to be sure that our new friends could at least eat once a day. The truth is that when someone becomes a friend, it makes a difference. We could not simply go home and rest easy knowing these remarkable leaders and new friends may not be eating while we were happily munching down cheeseburgers.

In 2010, after much prayer and consideration, Lori Martin, another Amahoro 2007 participant, and I realized that helping these communities become self-sustaining was the best way to be friends for the long haul. We formed the nonprofit African Road. In less than three years, the growing circle of African Road friendship has made way for the purchase of six acres of fertile land and a well for the orphans, a house for Steven and Providance's family and the twenty orphans who are part of their family, a livestock microenterprise and a literacy project (funded by American grade school boys Sam, Eli, Josh, and Will), sewing machines and training for the women's cooperative, a comprehensive health care initiative and annual medical insurance for each person Steven looks after, crafting businesses, a motorbike for Steven's back-road transport, a farming project to provide food for hungry orphans, cross-cultural pen-pal partnerships, sponsorship of education, seeds for widows' gardens, solar power, a regulation soccer field and youth sports program, including the first rural girls team in the area, and more. These goals came from the Rwandan communities themselves, not from our own best ideas of what we thought they needed. African Road has a responsibility to be sure we use funds with care and accountability, but we do not have to lead the way. We come alongside in efforts to help these friends become self-sustaining and we go forward together in friendship.

In Rwanda, women have been empowered, youth are starting businesses, kids who weren't eating each day now are. Because of transformative friendships, these women and children now have tools to build their own better future. Our trans-continental friendships deepen over time; we share stories and learn with and from one another, walk dusty red roads, eat beans and fried plantains together with our hands, cry, dance, pray, laugh, and celebrate. Friendship and partnership have changed lives on both sides of the world and built cross-cultural communities of connection and care. Short-term community has become long-term community for the good of the world, and more is to come.

Not everyone has the time, money, health, or inclination to travel internationally; however, everyone can connect to the story of a friend who does. I can invite my circle of friends in the US and beyond to come join me for a purpose. Because they trust my friendships and experiences, and they listen to and learn from the stories with which I am entrusted, they join in a global friendship that makes a difference, whether they travel or stand in supportive friendship from home. There are many ways that, together, we can build bridges. Being open to being transformed by others who live differently than we do not only helps change us but helps to connect and change the world.

Friendships have now taken me—and a good number of my friends—places we would never have imagined going. The African Road effort has in itself become a community, attracting non-goers (as well as goers and even people of other faiths) to this work that is attempting to follow the way of Jesus.

A True Hero

In more Christianized countries of Africa, church growth is king and the position of pastor is highly respected. Rwanda is one of these countries. The cultural sign of a healthy church is a bigger and better building to meet in, even in this country with a miniscule per capita income. Standing in front of an enthusiastic crowd and preaching a vigorous sermon is every Rwandese minister's dream. A small congregation in a humble building is better than no congregation or no building at all.

As a young man, my friend Steven Turikukiko felt called to become a pastor. There is no question that Steven has the heart of a true pastor, one who cares for the little ones, the weak, and the vulnerable. He is constantly surrounded by people in need who come to him because he is known to genuinely care. Despite his limitations financially, he will always do whatever he can to help someone in distress. In the span of one day he may share his household's limited food supply, find a spare place under a roof for someone to sleep, bring three more orphaned children into their family, help with a few dollars for medicine for a sick neighbor, seek a home for an abandoned infant, resolve twelve conflicts in the rural community of eighty orphans he cares for, petition the local school for mercy in allowing a child to stay in class without a uniform that fits, and perform a funeral for a woman who died of HIV/AIDS.

He spends each weekday looking after and encouraging along those eighty orphans, who are in child-headed households and who look to him as father. Sixty women, who are genocide survivors working together in a sewing and farming cooperative, call on him as brother and helper. The young mama with an infant who suffered brain damage during a routine medical procedure depends on him for the means to keep her baby boy alive. His two young children, along with the up to eighteen orphans he and Providence have folded into their home and family, eagerly await his return home each night. Still a young man at age forty, he's done this work for eighteen years now. His load is heavy but his heart is true. That is where his personal dilemma comes in.

Remember, Steven understood that God called him to be a pastor. And remember that in Africa being a pastor means leading a church congregation in a building with Sunday services, prayer services, Wednesday services, offering plates, powerful sermons, and passionate song and lively dance. To this end, Steven, ever an innovator, has planted at least a handful of churches in poor neighborhoods of Rwanda's capital city, Kigali, and in the rural villages of Kabuga and Gasogi. Although situated in humble settings, each of these simple, poor congregations has flourished and grown. Here's the catch: Steven is always looking for opportunities for others to use their gifts. To that end, every time he planted a church, he invited young pastors to join his team and help to lead these little congregations. In the meantime, Steven's reality is that he needs more hours than there are in a day to look to the needs of the eighty orphans in the village, the twenty children in his home, and the sixty women genocide survivors. With limited time to give his "new church," the young pastors inevitably need to take the lead, and eventually there is no longer need for Steven.

Now, in my estimation, what happened in these situations is a sign of great leadership—pave the way for young leaders to use their gifts and then step out of the way and move on to help others. Good leaders don't hold on tight and soak up the glory; they look for ways to spread the goodness and lift others up. To top that, no other pastor or leader I know of has personally done or even had what it took to make such a difference and be such a consistent presence for so many women and children over the years.

Think of this, between the orphans in his home, orphans in households headed by children, and the widows *and* their children in the village, over 250 women and children look to Steven for a way forward every day. Each one of them is surviving in large part because of Steven's love and sheer determination.

In conversation with Steven in May 2013, it came to light that because he has no recognizable church congregation to call his own, and because when people ask at what church he pastors and preaches he has no answer, he thinks of himself as a failure as a pastor. He confessed this with his eyes downcast and with a deep sigh. We were shocked. Steven, this man of small stature and huge heart, is a giant of a man in our eyes. He pours his life into pastoring a congregation—albeit scattered far and wide—that no one else would care for. People are literally alive and have hope because of his relentless love and care. He would not and could not turn from people in need or leave this life that has chosen him, but without a cultural framework to affirm his work, he still wonders if it really counts.

Without a building and a pulpit that others see, his work and his call are undervalued. It seems that sometimes the greatest heroes don't know they are heroes at all. Steven does not recognize what an astounding pastor he really is.

Steven practices the ministry of presence for others in his context. He may not have money, but he knows how to be with people in a way that brings hope. At the same time the ministry of presence is one of the most validating ways for friends to support Steven in his work. When we, friends from afar, take the time to come to meet him, to see his work, to listen to his stories, and come to love and care about the people he loves and cares for, it validates the significance of what God is doing through Steven's powerful, humble ministry.

African friends like to joke and tease me about me writing a book about being a Christian without going to church because the notion is so far outside of their cultural context. At the same time, I'd venture to say, my friend Pastor Steven is the most amazing Christian who doesn't go to church whom I've ever met.

Community and Connection

The person bundled in a blanket on a door stoop in Old Town is no longer a scary entity to be avoided; he is the very person I shared lunch with at Potluck in the Park last week. His name is Scott, he has kind brown eyes, and a scruffy dog named Scrap is his best friend. The compelling faces of African children are no longer nameless, overwhelming masses. They are individuals with unique stories, personal strengths, favorite foods, and specific challenges, and they have helped shape who I am today.

Transformational community can be produced by opening a picnic basket, traveling with a purpose, hosting a party for a good cause, or opening up to friendship with people on the other side of the world or people on the other side of the tracks in your own town. I wonder how this world might be shaped if we—the brave and the not-so-brave among us—all find some way, small or large, to learn about others. We can only begin to imagine what will happen when we step outside of our comfort zones with humble hearts, seek wise guides, and, importantly—whether we are in our own backyard, in a soup kitchen, or on the other side of the globe—when we don't go it alone.

When we start to ask where we can learn and who we can invite to join us, transformative community and world-changing outcomes are in store. I've seen it happen time and time again. As a non-goer you can gather others and form communities of healing and transformation. Don't just give money; take some action and get others to join you, tell stories, learn about and encounter the lives behind the cause, throw a party and invite guests you might not normally invite. When we open ourselves to learn, we are better able to encounter God's world in all of its beauty and diversity. Cross-cultural friendships not based on charity or feel-good deeds but based on humility and real relationship change us and create something new. As non-goers we may find companions, teachers, encouragers, and leaders in previously unexpected places. It is no surprise that such relationships are transformative and can make a genuine difference in the world—Christ is there, and that is good news.

❯❯ Questions and Action ❮❮

1. In what ways have you been changed and transformed by people who come from another place, class, culture, or lifestyle than your own?
2. In what ways have you protected yourself from people who are from an unfamiliar culture or setting?
3. What cross-cultural experiences would you like to have? Why?
4. What cross-cultural experiences make you nervous to even consider? Why?

Part 3

NEW STRUCTURES

8

ALTERNATIVES

Some Practical "Now What?" Questions for Leadership and Pastoral Care

It is fair to ask the "Now what?" questions. I don't go to church: "So now what do I do when I need someone to pray for me in a time of crisis?" "What does spiritual leadership look like without a paid pastor around?" "Are there new models for leadership and learning that don't replicate old problems?" "How can we learn from and respect the past as we go forward?" This very practical chapter dives into these questions and more.

I Don't Go to Church, but I Still Want . . .

When we consider the full spectrum of services the church can offer and then consider how to make our way forward as non-goers without them, it might feel scary and overwhelming. The local church congregation is often expected to provide members with inspiring sermons, meaty Bible studies,

Sunday school for young children, youth groups for teens, encouragement for spiritual growth at all stages of life, a source for Christian friendships and accountability, inspiring worship through music, a spiritual setting for weddings, the blessing of baby dedications, someone to make hospital visitations and offer end-of-life pastoral care, the sacraments of Eucharist (communion) and baptism, the rituals of memorial services and funerals, trustworthy pastoral counseling, and more. Stepping away from the extensive, traditional, "cradle to grave" care a church and a pastor can provide raises important considerations.

In July 2013, Rachel Held Evans's CNN Belief Blog post "Why Millennials Are Leaving the Church" struck a nerve. Her words prompted an outpouring of affirming responses from people. A few days later, she issued a follow-up post, "Why Millennials Need the Church," making a clarification. Evans reassured her readers that she isn't a church hater and explains that, although she was for a time "spiritual but not religious," she has found that she needs church. She notes baptism, confession, healing, leadership, communion, confirmation, and union with Christ as reasons why Millennials actually do need church.

Not all non-goers will share Evans's sense that each of these is essential to living a life of faith. At the same time, some who may not go to church do continue to consider these traditions significant for *being* church and as important parts of their lives. Can these marks of being church be met by non-going Christians when there is no paid pastor, are no preset programs, or is no institutional structure? Are there new alternatives to carry these historical markers forward for future generations? I believe the answer is a resounding yes.

I am curious about ways these needs can be meaningfully met outside of church walls. When looking at Sunday school, youth group, pastoral and leadership roles, prayer groups, and faithful financial giving, I remember a question posed by my good friend and colleague Deborah Loyd. She asks, "What would it look like if Jesus showed up here, right here, right now?" Keeping her question in mind helps free me to think outside of the box.

What could these marks of being church look like if Jesus were physically present to create them with us? We may find that we don't even want to replicate the programs that churches provide. Christ is already at work, right here, right now, which means we have a pretty darn good resource right at hand as we make our way forward. Some non-goers will find organic ways to live out their faith and may not feel a need for these traditions. Other non-goers who do want some of these expressions of their faith incorporated in their lives may create alternative communities and new, simple structures to carry on. Read on and discover how some non-goers are finding their way.

Urban Abbey

A few years back I gobbled up *An Introduction to Ecclesiology: Ecumenical, Historical & Global Perspectives* by Veli-Matti Kärkkäinen, a book full of tasty samples of practical theology. Kärkkäinen's book includes references to the work of the now-late pastor and theologian Letty Russell. I was delighted to discover the theology of "church in the round" or "church 'round the table." A gathering around a kitchen table served as Russell's metaphor for a way of being Christian community. This theology of hospitality and welcome confirmed what I knew intuitively. A theology of church 'round the table means there is space for all of us. It is a spirituality of connection that does not admit divisions between the ordinary and the holy. It is a space that is created and held by leaders who know that they are made for people, not people for leaders.

My small intentional community, Urban Abbey, circles around a long table and ladles up steaming bowls of lentil soup prepared by Dan and Scott, the dinner duo of the week.

As we eat we make connection with each other and we remember how and where we have experienced God since our previous dinner together. The ancient Ignatian practice of examen is our guide. Around the table, one by one, we share our consolation and our desolation—the place we most connected with God during the week and the place we most clearly felt the absence of God. The book *Sleeping with Bread* led me into this practice years ago.[1] We began to practice our own form of examen with our kids. At home we call examen "good thing, bad thing." Exchanging the best and worst moment of the day makes for meaningful family dinner conversation as well as for spiritual community formation. Our Urban Abbey community gatherings are woven together with liturgy from *Common Prayer: A Liturgy for Ordinary Radicals* by Shane Claiborne and Jonathan Wilson-Hartgrove.[2] These rhythms help each of us to reshape and re-imagine our relationship to time, reality, and priority.

Although we don't enter the doors of a church building, we are connected to the deep wells of Christian tradition. The opportunity to come together and share liturgy and examen over a bowl of soup helps us all to stay the course. Our table is open, and from week to week a flow of friends and neighbors join in this post-congregational, liturgical moment.

Robert Webber, the late scholar and church historian, describes something of the nature of this shift with the helpful phrase "ancient-future." Rather than create something entirely new and reject the historical gifts of the faithful who have gone before us, there is in fact a renaissance of ancient Christian practices. Paired with new technology and less hierarchical forms of community, ancient Christian prayer practices, age-old hymns, chants, and liturgy are taking on new life and leading people forward in faith.

I mentioned Webber's phrase to my friend Tekle Belachew, a bright young theologian and doctoral candidate from Ethiopia. He said, "Oh yes, you must be referring to *sankofa*." Tek informed me that this "ancient-future" concept itself has origins in African wisdom. *Sankofa* is an Akan term (from Ghana) meaning, "We must go back and reclaim our past so we can move forward; so we understand why and how we came to be who we are today," or, "One must return to the past in order to move forward."[3] The evocative and whimsical symbol of *sankofa* is a bird with its head facing the opposite direction its body is facing. Even though the bird is advancing, it makes it a point to turn and look to its past to make a better future. Literally translated, *sankofa* means, "It is not taboo to go back and fetch what you forgot." The humble and respectful spirit of *sankofa* and the ability to embrace the ancient while living into the future will serve us all well no matter where we are going.[4] We non-goers will be wise to lean into *sankofa* as we go forward.

Pastoral Burnout

Pastors are the ones who receive a call in times of a family crisis, are summoned to pray before a surgery, prepare and deliver the weekly sermon, provide pastoral counseling, and may lead the church prayer group. They are expected to hold the vision for the congregation and make good plans for accomplishing that vision. Administrative responsibilities aside, this is a big job. When I read through a comprehensive list of all the responsibilities a pastor may carry, I first feel exhausted, and then I am prompted to offer a shout-out to the many faithful pastors and priests who spend every day meeting these congregational needs. Each and every one of these means of congregational care is important. But I think back to Matt Casper's question—"Is this what Jesus told you guys to do?"—and I wonder.

There was a time when pastors didn't have to be program managers and executive administrators and churches didn't try to meet every social need for every age group. A 2010 *New York Times* article reads, "Members of the clergy now suffer from obesity, hypertension and depression at rates higher than most Americans. In the last decade, their use of antidepressants has risen, while their life expectancy has fallen. Many would change jobs if they could." The article questions, "Why have so many members of a profession once associated with rosy-cheeked longevity become so unhealthy and unhappy?"[5] Websites like PastorBurnout.com tell the stories.[6]

Until the 1920s, the pastor was a *cura animarum*, the "cure of souls" or "curate"—a person who cared for souls by helping people locate themselves in God's greater story. A July 2013 *Christianity Today* article by Andy Crouch quotes Rob Bell, founding pastor of popular Mars Hill Bible Church in Michigan and now a performance artist, who, speaking to a large group of pastors at Duke Divinity School in 2010, asked, "Do you ever feel like you signed up for a revolution [when you went into ministry], but ended up running a corporation?"[7]

Equipping and Empowering—Leadership for the Journey

When non-goers tackle the question about what to do when we are not going to count on a pastor to do the work, it is helpful to remember that the New Testament instructs us that many gifts have been given to help nurture the body of Christ. Oftentimes a church structure is top heavy, with the pastor expected to fill more roles than any one person can or should. It's a big load to bear and a lot of power to be given to any one person. A multitude of gifts are given and needed so that everyone can have a purpose in the body of Christ. A combination of gifted leaders, free to practice all their gifts for the good of others, can multiply the manpower and womanpower to provide plenty of resources for people who are younger in the faith to be equipped and discipled. The bonus is that when people are free to focus on what they are gifted to do, they are more effective and they have a more joyful life.

My friend Arnie the mentor frequently laments churches that haven't effectively empowered and raised up leaders. He imagines a world where every mature Christian will use their gifts right where they are to equip others. Instead of taking the spotlight or filling roles they aren't gifted to fill, what if each one was purposeful to follow the model of Jesus and bring twelve others along with them? If they impart what they have learned through time and experience, the twelve will be strengthened and encouraged. The twelve can follow suit and bring another twelve along with them, and so it goes. In this way no one is sitting it out, all gifts are welcome, and the potential for building networks of strong, mature followers of Christ is terrific.

This model needs no infrastructure to keep multiplying. Think of the leaders and potential leaders who can be equipped and empowered. Think of the money saved in programs and salaries. Think of the beauty of learning that can take place, woven with relationship that is always dynamic and growing. This requires a great deal of intention on the part of all involved, but you might imagine what vibrant, active goodness this leads Christ followers into. You also can imagine the benefit for a world that is open to seeing the Good News really lived out.

Shared Leadership

Third Saturday Community—named thus for meeting for the better share of the day on the third Saturday of each month—evolved originally from a community that had been meeting in our home weekly for well over a decade. When we made the move from a weekly group gathering to a one-day-a-month gathering, I found myself as leader facing a new and unexpected high level of expectation on that third Saturday gathering. What was the unique experience each month going to be? The pressure was on, and my graceful, dearly loved community friends began to feel a bit consumeristic to me. I felt like each monthly gathering was being graded. I imagined everyone wondering if that was "worth" taking a whole Saturday for. No one was unkind, and while it was probably even more my own insecurity rather than an accurate read of their thoughts and feelings, whatever the case, a shift could be felt.

I pondered and prayed and proposed an experiment. What if we found a way to share leadership and, at the same time, build relationships and strengthen each other? I pondered how to create the opportunity for those who had leadership experience and at the same time make a way to train, equip, and empower some who felt they had nothing to offer or had no experience to draw from. What if there was a way to validate all sorts of gifts in community? We were already a group with many creatives, such as artists and musicians, attending, and we'd already taken turns bringing different elements of teaching and leadership, so this wasn't a big leap. But it seemed that, this time, we needed something more.

I proposed that we try a new approach for the next few months, an approach that went beyond just divvying up responsibility. We needed to form a new kind of community with a sense of corporate ownership for what we were in together. Here is the experiment I cooked up: Every month a new triad would form—generally including one person who was comfortable in a leadership role, one person who might be more hesitant, and then a third person in the mix. Each person in the triad would be expected to contribute only what they were comfortable offering, but they did need to contribute something. The responsibility of the person who was more comfortable with leadership was to be sure that they themselves didn't take over and that everyone could find a way to be involved. The several-month experiment turned into several years of functioning with rotating triads of leaders.

The triad members of the month would plan everything that would take place during our Third Saturday time together. They would meet together sometime early in the month to decide how they wanted to use the time on the third Saturday and what they each would contribute. Often the group of three people, although they met together in the larger group regularly, might not have spent much time together outside of Third Saturday meetings. The planning time provided an opportunity to build into their relationships. It gave shy people a small group in which they could speak up, be known, and be heard. It gave experienced leaders an opportunity to practice healthy leadership that benefited others and to put their expertise to use. Together the triad members would ask, "What is God up to in our lives or in the world right now? What is intriguing to each of us right now?" They'd find a point of common interest and build on that together.

Third Saturday gatherings included a bountiful potluck meal. The triad might identify a theme for the meal depending on the season of the year or their focus for the day. The theme would be announced in advance so everyone could plan a creative culinary contribution. The content of the day could vary wildly depending on who made up the triad team of the month. We had a fall harvest potluck with a theme of abundance and a vegetarian potluck paired with a theme of simplicity and justice for the day. A local foods potluck was accompanied by a study of agricultural metaphors in Scripture. The menu was comfort foods when we studied centering prayer and meditation on Scripture. "Bring your most creative dish" meals were a good match for art immersion day, as was an Ethiopian meal when we learned about maternal health in Africa.

A triad might present the theme of justice with a combination of a hands-on art experience, Scripture reading, and discussion pertinent to the topic, and then cap it off with a letter-writing campaign to government representatives. With a focus on the theme of abundance, we might spend an hour in improvised song—led by Donna, a gifted violinist and banjo player, with Teresa on the piano, then have a poetry recitation and journal our prayers and thoughts of thanksgiving. Another triad might have a member lead us in Lectio Divina (a reflective way of reading and listening to the Scripture) and another who had prepared a complementary music playlist with songs that are meaningful to them. We'd listen while collaging and then share how we felt God in the listening and creating.

The shift in dynamic was electric. I loved the experiment and looked forward to the third Saturday of the month with great anticipation again. I assumed the role of cultivator, making sure that the triad members had been able to connect and that they had what they needed to be successful while they planned their Saturday. I'd generally keep a little something up my sleeve to add to the day for a group with less content, and I'd provide the elements for communion and prayer. It was easy and fun for me, and satisfying for the group too. I saw the group immediately shift from that slight tone of consumer mentality that had unexpectedly crept in, to one of mutual support and enthusiasm.

Some months were better than others, but that didn't matter anymore. Now that everyone was in on the action and felt the sense of personal responsibility to lead the group on their particular month, they knew what it took to shape the day and how much heart and effort went into the preparation. They were excited to work with their triad and looked forward to sharing with Third Saturday. They were equally excited to be there the following month and experience what the next triad had prepared for the community. It was a delightful season and a serendipitous discovery. And it provided Third Saturday with nearly three years of creative, beautiful, collaborative experience and learning.

After three years of triad leadership, Third Saturday community was ready to find another pattern for our Saturday gatherings. The next shift took place with each person feeling a strong sense of belonging in a community they helped shape and with a new set of deeper relationships. We learned a lot in those three years of triad collaboration. This experience reinforced my belief that the Spirit shows up when we hold our attempts in the humble posture of experiment and when we take a risk to bring our simple offering to the table.

Good leaders will encourage people to look for what God is already doing. That leader will then help people access the resources needed to do what they are being called to do. This is the model used by the church started by Gordon and Mary Cosby, the Church of the Savior in D.C., which has borne such good fruit over the decades. Church of the Savior believes that each person has a calling—something God has planted in them to care about and take action toward. Leaders help to connect people who have similar callings and empower them to succeed in their own mission rather than in a church project. Heather Kirk-Davidoff is the Enabling Minister of the Kittamaqundi Community Church (a church in the tradition of Church of the Savior) located in Columbia, Maryland. She's a terrific leader and a good friend and inspiration to me. I asked Heather if she'd share some stories from her congregation that represent this wise tradition. She shared this:

> This past January, Judy, a member of the community, came to see me. She was kind of agitated. She had just seen a documentary at our local community college about human trafficking. She was really horrified by what she learned through the movie and wanted to show it at our church. I thought that was a great idea and helped her think through how to do that. I then asked her more about why she thought the movie had affected her so much. She was a bit reflective about it, but at this point she was mostly in "doing" mode, specifically intent on bringing the movie to the church.
>
> A few weeks later, I checked in with her. It turns out another friend of Judy's wanted to show the movie at her church too and now they were thinking of cosponsoring an event. In a few more weeks, this event really bloomed. The local police department was sending an officer to talk at the event and they had even found a woman who runs a safe house for women fleeing from sex trafficking to come and

talk too. Judy advertised the event at our small church and in the community—the turnout was fantastic—several hundred people attended.

I talked to Judy the following week. She was super excited and was now wondering what next steps she could take on the issue. "Judy," I asked her, "I'm wondering if you might be experiencing a call." She said she'd been wondering about that and praying about it. I suggested that before she start work on any of the projects that she was considering, that she take a week or two to very intentionally consider the question, "How is God calling me to respond to this issue?" We talked about how she might discern more about her call, and the difference between responding to a call and accomplishing a task. This conversation continued over the following several weeks. She eventually became the cofounder of a Howard County chapter of a national anti-trafficking organization and drew a number of other people into the work and raising the consciousness of our congregation around this issue.

Judy didn't wait for someone else to take action; she listened to what she felt God was telling her to do and then did it. Heather didn't take charge or assume responsibility for the idea. She simply asked Judy good questions and encouraged her to look for God in her emotional response to the issue of human trafficking. I could fill a book with the stories Heather can share about what can happen when people are open to hear and respond to God's calling in their life. She continued with one more account.

Anne, another Kittamaqundi Community Church member—probably in her late fifties, is a petite person about five one in height. Anne needed a part-time job. She found a position working for the local homeless shelter on a three-month initiative. It would be her job to do outreach to residents in our area who live in camps in the woods along Route 1, a state highway at the edge of our county.

People were aware that there were folks living in the woods, but no one was sure how many. It was up to Anne to find out how many people were living there and to make a positive connection with them. Anne found volunteers to help her explore the woods and meet the camping residents. Not particularly commanding in terms of her physical presence, she walked right into the woods and talked with all these long-term homeless guys (some of whom are really pretty rough characters). After meeting them and engaging them in conversation, she'd ask them for directions to other homeless camps and keep going. Her team ended up locating over twenty camps with two to seven people living in each one, *way* more than anyone expected. I should note that we live in the third wealthiest county in the United States (Howard County, Maryland).

Anne was really overwhelmed by what she witnessed. Unlike Judy, she immediately identified this as a call from God. But she was convinced that God wasn't just calling her personally. God was calling the *community* to respond to this need, and she knew [she] was called to facilitate that. It is a long story, but put simply, she began a ministry to this population. She first delivered lunches to the camps—for the purpose of building trust and establishing relationships. Then, she started to talk to them about their needs. She eventually gathered a group of the woodland campers together to brainstorm (I'm talking about a group of homeless folks). That eventually led to the establishment of the Route One Day Resource Center, staffed just about entirely by church volunteers from over forty different churches.

From the beginning of the work, Anne gathered a group of pastors and other church leaders to pray for the ministry and for the county. They got together monthly and did Lectio Divina–style Bible study because Anne felt it was a good way for people from different Christian traditions to discern God's will together. Anne followed her call. It's made a big difference for many people.

The approach the Church of the Savior has successfully encouraged their members to embrace can serve as a tried-and-true guide for non-goers. The Cosbys worked hard to keep their ministry decentralized, organic, and alive for decades.

Understanding calling and gifting was essential to that goal. Heather Kirk-Davidoff's heart to empower others and lead by empowering bears good fruit.

We non-goers can listen for a sense of call, join others with similar vision, ask each other good questions, and make room for everyone to use their gifts for the good of the world. In the process, we equip each other and God's dreams come alive. There is not "one right way" to go. With plenty of prayer, good comrades, and a good dose of intention, you can continue to let that question Deborah Loyd posed inform your steps forward: "What would it look like if Jesus showed up here, right here, right now?"

Pastoral Care

What do we do when the going gets tough and we need wise spiritual counsel and support? What about pastoral care for non-goers? Being a non-goer shouldn't be synonymous with going it alone or being under-resourced. Without a pastor to phone and to fill the need for care in difficult times, non-goers will need to be purposeful in their pursuit of individual growth and transformation and in building helpful support systems.

I have the blessing of periodically meeting for spiritual direction with Sister Loretta, a wise Franciscan nun who just celebrated her Golden Jubilee (fifty-year anniversary of taking her vows and living a life of service). Spiritual direction differs from psychology and counseling in its focus. It is more of a listening and discernment process rather than a counseling session. The intention of spiritual direction is not to solve a problem, but instead to look for God's activity within the problem and within the rest of the person's life experience. A spiritual director generally is trained and certified in the process of guiding directees. It's common for spiritual directors to offer sessions on a sliding scale to be accessible to directees of all income levels. Over the years my spiritual direction sessions have drawn me into a deeper relationship and peace with God in the middle of whatever I am experiencing in life. As a spiritual director, Sister Loretta doesn't offer advice but helps me to explore how God may be at work in my life.

When we seek out healthy support and tend to our own broken places, we are part of making the world a better place. Whether we've formed a small community with non-goers or we serve our neighbors right where we are, working through our pain and choosing to gain new tools for dealing with conflict and engaging in communication brings benefit to not only ourselves but to all our relationships. Regularly seeing a therapist or a spiritual director and connecting with spiritual mentors gives us perspective and wisdom to walk through grief or hard circumstances and to keep growing. We can also join with other non-goers in small communities of support and friendship, in small, authentic groups where we can more consistently be aware of what is going on in each other's lives and then reach out and offer comfort, wisdom, and prayer when needed. Non-goers will be wise to ask how we are equipping others and how we are accessing "pastoral" support for all arenas of life (not unlike the mentoring constellation process). We will benefit, our communities and relationships will benefit, and, ultimately, the world will benefit when we pastor each other and when we recognize and value all the equipping gifts. There are so many ways that tradition, theology, discipleship, pastoral care, and spiritual formation can be held without the container of the institution and without discarding the essentials of faith.

We have a rich legacy in church history to draw from as we make new ways forward and answer the "Now what?" questions together. By sharing leadership, tending to our own broken places, being attentive to care for others, making space for prayer, and pursuing growth, non-goers can continue to add to the rich legacy of Christian tradition and in doing so be church in a way that spreads blessings far and wide.

⟫ Questions and Action ⟪

1. What are (or would be) the "Now what?" questions for you without the structure of church?

2. What is your favorite idea for an approach to leadership from this chapter? Why?

3. In what ways do you find support for and work on your personal, emotional, and spiritual health? In what areas do you need to find support for growth and health? List these, and then begin by finding one resource this month.

9

MONEY, MONEY, MONEY

Alternative Economy

We all probably think about money in one way or another every day. It shapes our lives more than we might care to recognize. It is worth asking how non-goers can support each other in alternative economies, rethink our giving and our work, and choose simpler ways of living that support more sustainable ways of being, in our own lives and in this world. This chapter offers practical suggestions for relating to money as non-goers.

No Offering Plate

When it comes to church and money, we may be accustomed to placing a check in the church offering plate as it passes by. Some people give to their church with a traditional tithe (10 percent) on their income. Others give what they can or give when it works out. In most churches we probably don't expect anyone to ask us direct questions about our money, our giving, or our spending. A congregation may have a building campaign or a mission project its members are asked to give to, but for the most part, finances remain a personal matter. I'd like to suggest that for non-goers, money—how we use it and how we earn it—can be reframed from "tithing" to finances integrated with faith. How do financial considerations affect our freedom to serve? How can we give wisely and practice generosity as people of faith? Can our use of money make a difference in the world?

The Scandrette family of ReImagine Community, an intentional Christian community in San Francisco (see chapter 13 for more on intentional communities), recently wrote a book that shares some practical answers to these questions. They share how they have dealt with their money for years as non-goers. *Free: Spending Your Time and Money on What Matters Most* is a collection of tried-and-true exercises for people who long for financial freedom, want to live generously, and may feel stuck where they are in relationship to money. Last week Mark, Lisa, and their nineteen-year-old daughter, Hailey, shared about their newest book with a roomful of friends in a North Portland coffee shop. Their message was provocative and energizing at the same time. I wish I would have had such visionary and winsome guides when I was a young person.

The Scandrettes note that, while the US is one of the world's richest countries, nearly every American feels financially stretched no matter what their faith orientation is. Mark and Lisa speak to matters of money, stuff, and time with the credibility of a family who, although they live in one of the most expensive cities in the world, has managed to live contentedly on a modest income and remain debt free. Lisa explained that in this country, though we have so much, we still tend to live with a chronic feeling of never having enough and always being behind. She pointed out that when we shift our thinking from that sense of "not enough" to a belief that together we can have enough, we become happier and more generous people. To change our money habits we first need to reorient our money perception.

The message the Scandrettes have to share isn't simplistic or guilt inducing. The exercises in their book are not designed for indiscriminate disposal of possessions or slicing and dicing our budgets to achieve some spartan outcome. Instead they offer an invitation: discover what really matters most to you and evaluate if how you spend your time and money is helping you to live out those values. When we are financially free we are more able to respond when we sense what our call may be—where and how we can serve in this world.

ReImagine Community members commit to doing what is even more uncomfortable than talking about one's sex life in a group—they talk about their money. Everyone shares information about what they earn and their monthly budgets. They share what they value, and they can invite the community to help them move toward those values. Interestingly, incomes of ReImagine people cover a broad span, some with hefty six-figure incomes and homes of their own (no small thing in San Francisco), some who are unemployed or underemployed and are couch surfing, and others who land somewhere in between. Each one is willing to hear from others and make changes when they are ready—and they understand that the changes probably won't look the same for everyone.

The process sounds scary but holds powerful potential for positive change. More money freed up leaves more money to be shared with others or invested in causes we care about or feel called to support. Most important, we can move away from the "always behind" feeling of scarcity toward spending our time and money on what matters most—we are free to choose.

New Models

What could sustainable ministry models look like for non-goers? How can ministry take place when there's no congregation to cover a monthly paycheck? Some non-goers and even pastors of small churches are beginning to think that bi-vocational ministry may be the way of the future. For people who want to be in touch with their neighbors rather than confined to working within the walls of a church, finding a job that puts them in touch with people is a solution. For women and men who are launching new ministries and don't intend to count on or even have a congregation to pay their salary, finding a job that provides flexibility is the way forward.

Some small communities of non-goers pool money and provide a small stipend to a community member to serve in a chaplain-like/cultivator role for the community. Others contribute money to a fund on a regular basis to fund community expenses (meals, child care, art supplies, retreats, speakers). Some pool all their money and share a "common purse," where each person in the community receives a share of the fund to live on. Others share possessions to cut back on consumption and spare the expense of purchasing infrequently used items.

Non-goers can commit to encouraging each other in simplicity and living modestly so they can work fewer hours and have more time to give to what matters to them. Some choose a career path that is well compensated but then choose to work fewer hours rather than accumulate more. Others choose work that is meaningful and connects to their mission and calling. Not all meaningful work is well compensated financially, but the satisfaction that comes from contributing to the world and doing what one has a passion for is the trade-off.

To this end, more and more, non-goers are engaging in business ventures that care about a triple bottom line or that are nonprofit ventures designed to provide an income but then to give back. The term "triple bottom line" was coined in the mid-'90s as a new measurement of what constitutes real profit for a business. The first measure is familiar—the "profit and loss account" bottom line. The second measurement is the "people account." The people account measures how staff, people in manufacturing facilities a business may contract with, and customers are treated. The third measure is the "planet account"—how environmentally responsible is the business. A 2009 *Economist* magazine article about the three "Ps"—profit, people, and planet—puts it this simply: "What you measure is what you get, because what you measure is what you are likely to pay attention to."[1]

Scott and Jolynn Davison opened the Arbor Lodge, a coffee and community space, with this in mind. The Arbor Lodge is situated in the North Portland neighborhood the Davisons live in. They recognized that there were very few coffee shops in a walk-able or bike-able range. They opened the Lodge as a mission or gift to the neighborhood. The Davisons generously make the space available for community events. They sell only locally sourced products, and as their website explains, "As a mission based business, profitability and social responsibility are weighed out in every decision."[2]

They may not be quite the same as non-goers, but the website of alternative church The Oregon Community heralds a banner reading "Church Is Empty" to emphasize their practice of getting outside the walls of church to meet and serve and know their neighbors. Once a month they even have an "empty service" where they serve rather than gather.[3] Ryan Saari, Oregon Community leader, is also founder of the Oregon Public House in Portland. With a mission of "Have a pint, change the world," the pub raised over three thousand dollars for charity in the first six weeks of operation in 2013. The Public House website describes the unique brewery:

> Oregon is the craft brewing capital of America and supports an extensive, thriving pub culture. Portland also hosts more non-profit organizations per capita [than] any other city in America. Our vision is to leverage these two unique attributes of our city by creating a family-friendly pub environment where our neighbors from the surrounding area can come to enjoy community around good food and craft beer while

supporting great causes. To integrate this vision of pub with benevolent outreach, we have established relationships with a number of non-profit organizations to which our pub will donate 100% of net profits. The customer will purchase their food and/or beverage, and then have a chance to choose where they wish their individual proceeds to go from a short list of local charities. We've simply positioned ourselves to be the "fundraising department" for these charitable organizations, by providing the community with great food and great beer in a warm, inviting environment. This ground-breaking model for business is literally the first of its kind and we believe this could begin a new wave of business and mission that has the possibility of changing the way we work, spend, and care for our communities. In addition, The Oregon Public House will be a place where people in the community can learn more of these outstanding non-profit organizations and discover practical ways they can become involved in transforming our world and improving the lives of others. We see our Pub as a community center for change and action where others can come to not only enjoy great food and drink, and give a little to the charity of their choice, but also learn how to take action and start to "be the change they wish to see in the world."[4]

Coffee and microbrews are the quintessential Pacific North-west combination. Add bikes and earth-friendly modes of transportation and you have the perfect trio. Vancouver, Washington, sits just across the river to the north of Portland. It is the home of intentional community Arnada Abbey. This tiny spiritual community is being supported by a peppy little business they formed called Eco Mopeds. Eco Mopeds are battery operated and charge overnight. They are designed to get people around without the expense of a car or motor-cycle. They do not require insurance or a license to operate. Arnada and Eco Moped founder David Knudtson shared his vision with me.

Year one we imported 4 units as test units. Year 2 we sold 43 units basically only in the Portland, Oregon, area. So far this year we have sold over 60 units and summer just really hit! Our goal is to help lots of people in similar spiritual communities sell this great product and support their communities. Imagine for a moment if 350 metro areas had 350 new outposts for the Kingdom of God and they were fully supported by the sale of Electric Bikes.[5]

Sustainable transportation for sustainable community—a pretty nice pairing.

What if we non-goers encouraged each other to find our way toward the freedom to spend time and money on what matters and then support one another in making lifestyle changes to reach these goals? Creating businesses and nonprofits for meaningful work and connection to the neighborhood and the world and shifting beliefs about money will free us to give more, in a way that matches our values, and with a light heart. We move beyond the paradigm of just giving money to becoming part of a larger and more meaningful story of connection and transformation.

⟩ Questions and Action ⟨

1. What matters to you most? How are you living out those values with the way you use your money?
2. What might be the benefits practically, emotionally, and spiritually in simplifying your lifestyle?
3. What would be the challenges to simplifying?
4. Is it comfortable or uncomfortable for you to talk openly about your own finances?
5. Think of at least one other person to join you in an honest exploration of finances.
6. What advantages might there be to making financial shifts with a community of others rather than on your own?

WITHOUT THE CONTAINER

Alt-Study and Worship

Going forward without the ready-made container of the institution doesn't have to mean abandoning practice. To carry faith forward in our own lives, as well as for the generations to come, we need methods for learning and we need steadying ritual. As people exit church, they may seek alternatives to the containers they have long known. The slang word *alt* emerged from the alternative music—or "alt-music"—of the independent, underground rock scene beginning in the 1980s. This chapter explores possibilities for alt-study, alt-ritual, alt-worship, alt-prayer forms, and alt-preaching. The ideas and stories are simply seeds for inspiration. The sky is the limit as you discern with others what will best serve you, the time, the place, and the people right where you are.

Alt-Study

Years of experience in the ready-made container of church Bible studies leave me a veteran of everything from the estimable "Bible Study Fellowship" program to Kay Arthur and Beth Moore series (yep, there was a time that I did those), R. C. Sproul, Experiencing God, Serendipity Group Studies, Navigators material, and more. Women's Bible studies, young married group Bible studies, home fellowship group Bible studies—you name it, I've done it. I've been a participant and I have been a leader.

In both cases, my experience has been that people in church settings are often uncomfortable expressing a difference of opinion and study books are typically designed to prompt specific answers. Participants often prefer to be given answers to questions rather than probe for meaning. It is easier to cite what we like or don't like rather than delve into the personal implications for living life. Rarely is there a warm welcome for those who do think independently and are bold enough to ask the hard questions about what Scripture might be saying about how we spend money or how we use our power in the world or to cross-examine what a particular passage may mean. A value for "answer-right-ism" tends to reign over a value for thoughtful "learner-ism." While the time and effort I put into these studies helped me gain some useful exegetical tools and an early familiarity with Scripture, ultimately, I felt obligated and constrained rather than inspired and enriched. I was hungry for alternatives long before I knew that might even be a possibility.

The historical institution of the church has been the keeper of traditions, practices, and doctrines of faith. It has generally been where people come to receive teaching and instruction and to meet with others for study and training in matters of faith. Faithful monastic communities transcribed Scripture before printing presses, and during times of persecution they safeguarded it. Catechisms and confirmations steeped children and young Christians in the particulars of the doctrines and beliefs of their church tradition, church Bible study groups helped people become acquainted with

Scripture, and weekly sermons provided a dose of inspiration and instruction.

As people of faith leave the institution of the church, one concern that is often voiced is what might happen without a container for consistent teaching and without a structure to encourage regular Bible study. Will the doctrines of the historical church go by the wayside? Will the beliefs and practices of Christians become willy-nilly, whatever goes? Will children grow up unformed and will new believers have no sense of how to engage Scripture in a thoughtful and well-informed way? In her helpful book *Christianity for the Rest of Us,* church scholar Diana Butler Bass raises caution about the way forward:

> In an age when people claim to be "spiritual but not religious," it is fashionable to downplay institutions in favor of direct experience of the divine. . . . Without some sort of architecture, spirituality cannot be sustained over time or taught to successive generations. At its best, structure carries life-giving wisdom beyond our immediate experience and limited memory.[1]

Bass makes a good point. Individualistic spiritual experience truly can be personally meaningful, but it doesn't carry forward well unless it is passed along and put into action. And that requires connection with others.

I am an introvert at heart. I love time alone to read and think. I have had significant times of connection with God when I am by myself. I meet God as I take in the expansive beauty and power of the sea; I can experience the Spirit as I sit in my favorite chair to pray and think. All the same, I know I also need to be connected to others. I need to be part of a learning community.

"And let us consider how we may spur one another on toward love and good deeds, not giving up meeting together, as some are in the habit of doing, but encouraging one another—and all the more as you see the Day approaching" happens to be a favorite Scripture verse.[2] It describes the synergy I feel when I sit with other people in animated and earnest inquiry, when we exchange ideas that relate to life and practice, asking and examining good questions together, exercising sound reason—and being moved accordingly to action. I have no stomach for pontification or the touting of personal expertise, but when humble stories are told and questions are asked, personal transformation and real-life action and application can come about. The open study of a thought-provoking book or the examination of a challenging passage of Scripture with a community of people willing to engage all perspectives and stop to listen to all involved . . . now *this* is good food. This is Bible study at its best, and indeed, I have not often found it to take place in church settings.

In addition to group Bible study, there is value in sound scholarship and thoughtful teaching offered by people who have expertise in biblical studies and theology. Good preaching is an art and can be a gift to community. Let it be noted, though, that going to a church event and listening to a sermon does not constitute being church together. For non-goers, when it comes to preaching, there are a growing number of options to Sunday morning sermons. Less passive consumption and more active intention is required to learn this way, but a variety of options, including podcasts, special speaker events, books, classes, people's seminaries, and even new kinds of community forming with seminary-trained people are possibilities for receiving theological and scriptural instruction.

Beit Midrash

In Hebrew, *beit* means house and *midrash* comes from the word root that means "to seek, to search out, to dig for meaning."[3] I am fascinated by Beit Midrash—houses of digging for meaning. Very cool.

In his book *Searching for Meaning in Midrash*, the late Rabbi Gershon Schwartz declared, "If we define midrash as 'homiletic or legal interpretations of the Bible,' that is, interpretive readings of sacred text, then the process of midrash certainly continues today . . . and can be 'done' by Christians, as well as by Jews."[4] Jewish historian Micah D. Halpern writes:

> [Jewish debate] . . . forces interaction. The rabbis warned of the dangers of learning alone. They demanded that one find a study partner. A traditional learning interaction is filled with energy and dialogue, debate and discussion and the page comes alive as the commentators become active participants in the discussion and the learning partners actually speak to the text as if it is alive . . . Conversations are lively, loud and filled with gesticulations and frustrations. Jewish debate takes place in a *Beit Midrash*, a study hall. Unlike our contemporary libraries where silence resounds, Jewish schools are filled with noise. The *Beit Midrash* is a room or building packed with books, people, noise and tumult. According to the dictates of Jewish debate, even when alone in the study hall, one studies out loud. The student reads text aloud—sometimes even in different voices with actions emphasizing important points until the arguments are clear and it is the norm to spend months on a single page of Talmud or text.[5]

Instead of abandoning the foundations of faith and losing the desire to learn, grow, and mature, many non-goers actually have a deepening desire for authenticity, an earnest pursuit of growth, and faithfulness to Scripture. We can learn from Beit Midrash and the long-standing tradition of lively inquiry and dynamic approach to study. As Rabbi Schwartz suggests, it is indeed possible for Christians to create space for a sort of "Beit Midrash" and engage participants in creative, multidimensional thinking and query. In fact, honest inquiry, thoughtful study, engaging the text "as if it is alive," and serious doctrinal discussions are already popping up in some unexpected places for non-goers.

Microbrews and Microstudies

The worn wood slab table at the Lucky Lab Brew Pub on the busy corner of North Killingsworth and Concord is crowded with a gathering of women and men. They are young and not-so-young non-goers, seminary grads with tattoos, old guys in flannel shirts, young social workers, along with a neighbor or two. They all engage in lively banter and earnestly take turns listening and sharing their own thoughts and questions. They might be examining a passage from Isaiah or reading from the works of Augustine.

While holding a value for understanding the contribution of historical church practices, these non-goers bring with them the need for room to doubt, a preference for shared leadership, and a desire to engage in practical acts of spiritual formation. They see the life of faith as a journey rather than a destination. This approach makes more room for questions and difference of interpretation and opinion. When there is a commitment to create this kind of safe space, some forms of study that have become weary in the institutional church can take on new life. Portland, Oregon's Red-Letter Pub nights and Theology on Tap in various cities are study groups, meeting regularly in local brew houses. Theology in the neighborhood nights, early morning Psalms readings, Lectio Divina in a living room (the ancient Christian practice of meditation on a passage of Scripture), and book studies that link Scripture and spiritual formation are percolating up in bars, coffeehouses, and neighborhoods around the country.

I met August "Gus" Kroll, founder of a People's Seminary in Portland, Oregon. People's seminaries have been popping up in the US as a way of making theological education and engagement accessible to everyone. Gus put it this way, "I couldn't just sit in pews [anymore] when I am hearing things I disagree with over and over." Gus founded the Portland People's Seminary in late 2011. "I love books. That's how it all started. Friends who were in seminary would tell me, you have to read this. Not only did I learn from the books my friends passed along, I also learned that they were wrestling with huge debts when they graduated. I got tired of reading books by myself but I knew I wasn't going to go to seminary."

Thus the seeds for People's Seminary were planted. Now a group of young people meet monthly at the McMenamins Barley Mill Pub to study theology and books about the Christian life together. After eighteen months of experience, Kroll is asking practical questions. He wonders how we can move from exchange of mental, cerebral information to active engagement. He's also asking what can be done about people he describes as having "more bark than bite," meaning those who may think they have something worthwhile to say but have not studied the material.

His remark brought to mind one of those classic Bible studies that I participated in years ago—the venerable Bible Study Fellowship. One firm tenet of BSF is that anyone who has signed up to participate is always welcome to come, but unless they have completed the reading and the study assignments, they need to be listeners rather than contributors. I think they were probably on to just what Gus was frustrated with here. His third question holds interesting potential as we move into the future: "What might it look like to grow a pastor organically?" An organic pastor would be educated with no debts and no obligations to denomination and, therefore, free to serve in the slums or from his or her own back porch.

Guest speakers with expertise have given lectures to bring topics alive and bring sound perspective. A few months back the students selected the book *Practicing the Way of Jesus: Life Together in the Kingdom of Love* by my friend Mark Scandrette (also coauthor of the book about money in the previous chapter). The book includes practical assignments to help us be formed in our hearts and with our bodies, as well as our heads. Gus got in contact with Scandrette and asked if he would consider doing some live video conferences with the seminary class. Scandrette agreed as long as the class would commit to six weeks' time to read the book and complete the exercises. The seminarians jumped in and were glad they did.

I guarantee that Gus isn't the only one asking such questions or making forays into the future of learning and education. Just watch and see what the future brings.

Tierra Nueva

Chris Hoke describes himself as an over-churched, Southern California, third-generation missionary kid who left the church disenchanted with the whole package, wondering if and where God was at work in the world. After years of searching and study, Chris found himself drawn to the work of Tierra Nueva.

Tierra Nueva was founded in 1994 in rural Burlington, Washington, by Bob and Gracie Ekblad. The Ekblads have a long-term commitment to working with people on the margins and to deep practical and theological engagement with the sociology of poverty. They first lived and worked with the poor for seven years in Latin America, with an emphasis on soil conservation. Upon their return to the States, they formed Tierra Nueva to work with and build relationships with the migrant, gang, prison, and drug-affected community in the heart of agricultural Skagit Valley in northwestern Washington State.

Tierra Nueva, meaning "new earth" in Spanish, is home to the People's Seminary, formed to study Scripture and theology with people on the margins of society. The Tierra Nueva website describes the purpose of the seminary this way:

> God is most fully revealed in Jesus' descent from a position of power and privilege to one of service and solidarity with the poor and excluded of his day. God meets us in our encounters with the vulnerable and the weak: inmates, immigrants, and other outsiders. God challenges, teaches and calls us through

our excluded neighbors. Unfortunately, there are more and more people who find themselves outside the Christian community, unable to participate in or benefit from the transformational power of God's Word. People marginalized due to race, social class, language, lifestyle, legal status often reach the conclusion that God is against them and that they are not welcome in the Church. Mainstream church people find few opportunities to authentically encounter people at the margins. Such fruitful encounters can transform the church's worship, ministries, theology and Biblical interpretation. Theological education is especially exciting when people from the mainstream and the margins come together and discover a Gospel that is real and visible, enabling both groups to discover their vocation, serving together as Christ's body in the world. The People's Seminary is an ecumenical learning center for scripture study and theology, rooted in active ministry in solidarity with people on the margins.[6]

As a grassroots community of people following Jesus and practicing radical grace, the work of Tierra Nueva includes advocacy for immigration rights, The Underground (a coffee roasting operation run by released felons), a family support center, a sustainable farming project, transitional homes for men coming out of prison, and "clean-and-sober" housing and transitional support for women. Tierra Nueva is knit together with a profound trust in prayer and the inspiration and direction of the Holy Spirit in each of these ministry areas.

Being part of the chaplaincy program at the county jail in conjunction with Tierra Nueva is what drew Chris back to Jesus. "The jail became my church—to worship with all these guys who knew how messed up they were. These skinny young gang bangers got what Jesus was about. These guys didn't try to dish up churchy answers. They were on the edges of their seats taking it all in. I was having better conversations than I ever had with my peers. We were praying, crying, and writing raps together. A whole bunch of felons and gang members welcomed me into their heart."

Chris shared a formative experience of exploring Scripture with his new friends in the prison:[7] "A few years ago I was looking at Matthew 22, the parable of the wedding banquet, with an influential gang member and meth dealer." (I'll call this man Carlos.) "Carlos really liked the introduction to this passage and demanded the entire pod come join us to hear the passage. Carlos told the guys in the pod, 'You would like this sh–t, homie.' And they came."

> Then he said to his servants, "The wedding banquet is ready, but those I invited did not deserve to come. So go to the street corners and invite to the banquet anyone you find." So the servants went out into the streets and gathered all the people they could find, the bad as well as the good, and the wedding hall was filled with guests.[8]

Chris continued, "As I read through the passage, Carlos stood and started interjecting, 'Check this out you f–ing bastards. It's like God coming to you! The church people don't get it—God wants *us* to fill his house, and—I am going to find all the other bad people like us.' Things took another turn with verses 11–14":

> But when the king came in to see the guests, he noticed a man there who was not wearing wedding clothes. "Friend," he asked, "how did you get in here without wedding clothes?" The man was speechless. Then the king told the attendants, "Tie him hand and foot, and throw him outside, into the darkness, where there will be weeping and gnashing of teeth."[9]

Chris shared what happened next: "Carlos really got angry about this. I could see it—he felt like he was sold one message but [it was] swapped for another. It was painful to see. Carlos was screaming, 'So, we think we are invited but then we find out we have to wear your stupid wedding clothes. You will tie us up and throw us in the darkness!' It was really clear to see that Carlos took Scripture more seriously than we do."

When Chris shared this scene with me, I was startled. Pondering my own response, I realized that I had always considered myself as someone who had been invited to dinner in the second round, not seeing myself as someone who might have been in the privileged first round who declined their invitation. At the same time I had never doubted that I would be naturally welcome to stay for dinner when I did arrive. And I hadn't really given much thought to the guy who was kicked out. I'd just focused on the message of inclusion *for myself.* I also realized that I'd spiritualized the wedding clothes. I suppose I'd figured that maybe the guy who got kicked out hadn't had his heart in the right place—for me the "wrong clothing" indicated that there was a problem with the state of the guy's heart. That meant that I'd assumed, of course, that my heart was in the right place. When Carlos heard the text, he instantly saw himself as the one with the wrong clothes, the one who did not belong, and the one who would be thrown out and cast away. Carlos, from his different social location than mine, made me look at the text in a completely new and rather uncomfortable light. Chris was right when he said that Carlos took Scripture more seriously than I did.

When we take seriously the perspective and wisdom of oppressed peoples, when we view Scripture through their eyes, the tables can flip on us—"who's in and who's out" takes on a whole new meaning. Passages that may have grown dull with familiarity take on a new, sharp edge. We may be forced to step back and take a second look at our assumptions. Tierra Nueva creates space for people from all walks of life to come together, give and receive grace, see through new eyes, and in the process be transformed. The interaction with Carlos brought this home for Chris. And for me too.

Women's Theology Group

The shady backyard of my funny, smart, tattooed friend Pam Hogeweide, author of *Unladylike: Resisting the Injustice of*

Inequality in the Church, serves as a school for women's theology. Pam convenes female pastors and seminary professors to teach, and then she invites a diverse group of women to attend quarterly women's theology groups in her neighborhood. Growing numbers of ordinary women, who might never have thought to read theology on their own or to step into a seminary classroom to see Scripture through a new lens, come together to do some serious study and engage in deep discussion. Many women are relieved and empowered to discover that Jesus came not to limit and restrict women but to free them to serve in all capacities. These women are exploring Scripture and good theology to understand more clearly how liberating the ways of Jesus are. The learning environment Pam creates isn't permanent, but the learning that takes place is. You can bet that once these women complete their theology courses, they will pass along what they have learned to their children, their friends, and others they influence and lead.

No Teacher, No Preacher

In addition to group Bible study and learning communities, there is value in sound scholarship and thoughtful teaching offered by people who have expertise in biblical studies and theology. Good scholarship is a gift to community, and preaching can be an art (think of Martin Luther King Jr.'s sermons). Sermon preparation can take several days of study, writing, prayer, and reflection. It's a weighty job for sure. We've all heard fabulous expositors and we've all been bored as can be by other sermons. Going to a church event and listening to a sermon does not constitute being church together. No matter the case, here's the rub: most sermons may not make that much difference in the long haul. Now, perhaps your life was dramatically changed by a sermon you've heard, or maybe you at least remember the sermon from last week (*if* you heard one last week). On the other hand, chances are, like most people, you aren't too likely to have had one imprinted on your memory.

Now don't get me wrong. I like learning from people who are well versed in their area of expertise—whether that's in church, a university, or cooking class. Heaven forbid we have a world full of people who all think they are resident experts on topics they haven't sweated and labored to learn. However, one person preparing for hours each week to deliver thirty minutes of expository teaching on a Sunday morning was probably not on the list of what Jesus had in mind when he sent the Spirit to empower us all as ministers. The preaching pastor model might actually serve to disempower rather than empower congregants who become passive listeners but not seekers and students themselves.

Pastor and author Doug Pagitt's *Preaching Re-Imagined* is a simple little book well informed by community life at Solomon's Porch in the Twin Cities. Pagitt has explored alternatives to the ordinary approach to sermons. He chalks up the problem with preaching to a problem of relationship with the hearers and what he calls "speaching"—the combination of a speech and preaching that directs information at the listener and automatically confers more authority to the pastor/preacher, elevating him or her above the congregation. He engages his community in what he calls "progressional dialogue." Progressional dialogue trusts that the people have something to add. It believes in the priesthood of all believers. It invites interaction and doesn't rest on declaring definitives but on offering perspective: "The Bible becomes part of our conversation, not a dead book from which I extract truth."[10] Like the study model of midrash, exploration of Scripture becomes lively and full of possibility for each person. It encourages a relationship with the Bible and deepens the connection with God. Three cheers to leaders who engage everyone in lively dialogue, ask discomforting questions, and find practical ways to encourage action, engagement with the text, and empowerment.

All that goes to say, there's a good case to be made for non-goers not fretting about the lack of a weekly sermon. Active engagement and communal responsibility take the place of reliance on a sole authority figure to dish up a message, translate meaning, and dictate direction. This approach to exploring Scripture and theology can incorporate well-regarded resources from a variety of perspectives and ultimately invite a deep level of trust in the work of the Spirit in community.

Rituals and Rites Revised

When it comes to the ceremonies, rituals, and other significant events in life that we have traditionally depended on the church to provide, we may need to chart a new course as non-goers. Although sacrament and ritual might look a little different outside of church, they remain important to many non-goers. Finding creative alternatives and shifting the context does not diminish the meaning of rites of passage and spiritual sacraments.

One of my favorite weddings ever was that of Rich and Marbry Walker. Rich and Marbry were part of the Third Saturday Community when they married. I'd followed their story of meeting and dating and rejoiced when they became engaged. I had the joy of officiating their ceremony in my cozy living room as they stood surrounded by a circle of friends on a cool, late-winter evening. Marbry looked beautiful in her simple teal dress, chosen with every intention of wearing it again on other occasions. Rich looked sharp in jeans and a blazer and sporting Converse high-top shoes. The vows were tender and personal. Teresa, a jazz composer friend, sat at our upright piano and improvised softly through the ceremony. Candles of blessing were lit by everyone present, prayers were prayed, and toasts were raised in that circle. The ceremony continued as the guests joined Rich and Marbry for a delicious dinner of curry chicken, followed by beautiful homemade citrus wedding cupcakes. Another group of friends generously provided the meal. At the end of the evening, the newlyweds were whisked away by a Yellow Cab (the Walkers own bikes rather than a car). The Walkers committed their marriage to God and spoke aloud their intention to live lives of meaning and intention in this world together, beginning with no debt from their wedding. I can to this day attest to the fact that the Walkers are indeed living out their declaration to build their lives with intention and care.

Baptism is a significant marker in the Christian life. I've known hot tubs to become excellent baptismal tanks, and rivers can work just fine too for baptism by immersion (think *O Brother, Where Art Thou?*). A backyard fountain or beautiful bowl of water can become a font for infant baptism. Sometimes non-goers will assemble with other non-goers in a small community to share in the sacraments of communion or baptism. Others will conduct these in their own homes as an act of faithfulness. Most non-goers understand themselves to be part of the priesthood of all believers and accept responsibility and authority for administration of the sacraments. Occasionally a small assembly of non-goers might prefer to incorporate a member who is an ordained minister to fulfill these functions when the occasion arises. While this person might not lead the gathering or bear ongoing pastoral responsibility, they could serve as an ecclesial representative for sacraments—serving communion or performing baptisms. Roman Catholic communities tend to maintain a strong connection to parish church for the sacraments and rites, although even then, more and more frequently communion is served by women or men who are designated as "extraordinary ministers of the Eucharist."

The faith forms of non-goers do not need to be small or self-centered. The gospel survived the catacombs, and the persecuted church in the former USSR and China carried forward essential creeds and practices in their small, scattered gatherings without an authorized container or visible structure. In the same way, I believe we can trust that God can work through the growing number of small, scattered expressions of Christian communities and faithful non-goers actively following Jesus and living vibrant lives of faith now. I believe there is evidence that faith will be sustained over time and taught to successive generations by the innovative communities being formed by non-goers who are intent on living in the way of Jesus.

Alt-Worship: A Good Dose of Smells and Bells

If I miss anything from participation in regular Sunday church services it is singing with larger groups of people. There is something about lifting voices in unison and singing strong, true words about God together that reaches me deeply. Although I miss this, occasionally singing a simple hymn with a few other people can carry me forward. For my husband, Ken, that absence of corporate worship in song is practically agonizing. He needs to get his whole self involved in his worship and he needs other people around him doing the same thing. While I like hymns and the occasional, thoughtfully composed song of worship by an innovative artist or getting lost in a classical composition, he loves contemporary pop-rock choruses, sentimental praise songs, and rhythmic gospel and soul. He is happiest when he can sing with all his heart and move with all his body. Although our personal preferences are distinct, I know we are not alone in missing this aspect of a "church worship service."

Non-goers all over the world have been creatively exploring alternative ways to gather and worship beyond traditional church services. They range from neighborhood living rooms to cathedrals in the hearts of great American cities, and they draw on experiences from music to meandering walks in the woods. There are many examples of post-denominational liturgical gatherings, and many more will be created in the future. All over the Western world, liturgy and art, tradition and innovation are being melded to craft creative post-church and post-denominational alternative worship gatherings. No longer is the container of a weekly church service or the organizational structure of a denomination the only place to find points of convergence and connection where scattered saints can periodically gather and share in meaningful corporate worship. In our years as non-goers, we have found myriad experiences of corporate worship and contemplative communal space to nurture our spiritual lives. And, along the way, we have found many friends and kindred spirits. Here are some of these stories.

God Space

The darkened interior of the stone cathedral pulsed with deep, resonant tones and shifting lights. An array of gifted musicians, each absorbed in producing their part in a carefully crafted collage of electronic and acoustic sounds, were scattered about on the chancel. The sound was at turns haunting, inviting, energizing, and stirring. Poignant readings and sections of silence punctuated the rhythm of the evening. The spirit was holy and solemn, and the people in pews were captivated and drawn in. I found myself moved to tears by the beauty and creativity reflecting God's majesty.

Urban Hymnal, also called the Opiate Mass, was created as an experiment designed to address the needs of non-goers like ourselves as well as people who might not ever choose to attend an ordinary church service. A grant from the Calvin Institute of Worship helped to fund these gatherings held in a rotating variety of old cathedrals in the Seattle, Washington, area. The effort was a collaboration between three congregations, exploring "how new, creative, relevant music, text, and art can help people pray more honestly, engage more deeply with one another and address the needs of the community."[11] One of the stated goals was to provide an opportunity for smaller communities of Christians to come together for a larger worship gathering. The musicians who wrote the original music and coordinated and led the Urban Hymnal found "this was a way to worship and engage with God without the typical boundaries of a Sunday service imposed on our craft."[12] The Hymnal was designed to "create a transcendently beautiful worship experience . . . expressing both the whisper-quiet voice and the epic-grandeur of God."[13] It worked for me, and from what I could see, it did for the many others who'd come together that evening as well.

Beer and Hymns

In some contrast to the subdued and transcendent spirit of Urban Hymnal, my friends Angie and Todd Fadel of Portland, Oregon, craft a quarterly "Beer and Hymns" meet-up for a growing contingent of people who don't find themselves at home in a traditional church setting. Angie's rich, earthy, and soulful voice paired with Todd's energetic and excellent musicianship combine with their pastor-hearts and creative vision as they lead a ragtag and diverse crowd in a heartfelt, loud-voiced, good theology, old-time hymn sing, along with foamy mugs of great Portland brew. A large downtown church with which the Fadels have no formal affiliation makes a fellowship hall available for this raucous and holy gathering. I've been able to dip into these warm and deeply worshipful sessions a few times, and I've left better for joining in.

Taize

Taize has been a longtime oasis for me and for many of my non-goer friends. For twelve years I led my Third Saturday Community, along with a smattering of other non-goers, on monthly pilgrimages to Taize services at Lewis and Clark College, a local liberal arts college. Sister Loretta, a Franciscan sister, and Reverend Mark, the Protestant campus chaplain, collaborated to host a First Friday prayer service that drew people from all over the Portland metropolitan area to join in the chants and shared silence for which Taize services are known.

Taize was born in Taize, France, in 1940, soon after the start of the Second World War, with a hope to "offer a possible way of assisting some of those most discouraged, those deprived of a livelihood."[14] In the aftermath and regret of the war, it became an ecumenical movement fostering peace and justice through prayer and meditation. The distinctive Taize worship services and an international, ecumenical Taize community sprouted up in France but spread all over the world, now with communities in more than thirty countries and countless gatherings using Taize worship and prayer. Not connected to a church, denomination, or tradition, but simply to Christ and the values of kindness, simplicity, and reconciliation, Taize, France, has become a destination for spiritual pilgrimage for over one hundred thousand young people each year. All around the globe Taize prayer services are held on university campuses, in chapels and parks, in pubs and in schools. The ecumenical spirit of Taize along with the simple, reassuringly predictable yet meaningful liturgy make it possible to easily gather followers of Jesus who may have never met and to join voices in quiet, reflective songs and in chants and prayers for peace and healing in this world and in our own lives.

Non-Goers Here, There, and Everywhere

The UK and Australia, in their deeply post-church contexts, paved the way for a movement that is growing across the Western world. With names like Moot, Host, Grace, iKON, and Feast, artists and musicians come together to craft worship environments and experiences. Experienced alternative worship curators and leaders such as Sue Wallace, Mark Pierson, and Jonny Baker have led the way, beginning as early as the late 1980s and early 1990s. London-based Moot describes itself as "a living sign that those who may not relate to traditional or contemporary expressions of church can find a spiritual path within the Christian contemplative tradition."[15] Moot regards "the inspiration of scriptures and saints, monastics and mystics, philosophers and artists throughout the centuries, and seek[s] to offer generous hospitality and open conversation to all."[16]

For Moot and other alternative worship and post-denominational liturgical communities and gatherings, denominational and theological lines give way to room for difference. The belief that God is active and present everywhere—in culture, in secular society, in the creative process, and in creation—means that life is not divided between the sacred and the secular. In the words of Steve Collins of Grace UK alternative worship community, "If this is so then the visible Church is not the only potential place to encounter Christ."[17]

These are hands-on, participatory places where no passive consumption is allowed and where leadership is understood as "re-empowering people who think they have nothing to offer . . . that fits within the confines of a conventional church event."[18] Alternative worship and post-denominational liturgical leaders may or may not be ordained or paid, and a community or an event is more likely to be "curated" than overtly led. This means that the organizer or convener identifies and gathers others to work together. The curator guides a process so that the result is cohesive, and he or she does not need to be a dominant or visible leader. This kind of leadership is fluid and nonhierarchical with a value for the gifts of all rather than elevating the gifts of preaching, teaching, and musicianship. The purpose of post-church liturgical and alternative worship communities is not to draw people into existing churches or to reach a particular group or to make Christianity seem cool. The purpose is to create a unique opportunity for people to connect with God.[19]

In 2004, I met Mark Pierson of Cityside, New Zealand, at the Worship, Arts, Liturgy, and Preaching in an Emerging Context conference at Asbury Theological Seminary in Lexington, Kentucky. In my role as coordinator for communications and worship stations for the conference, I was eager to trade notes with others who were pioneering in crafting alternative worship spaces. Mark was considered the guru of alternative worship events and short-term interactive Stations of the Cross installations. He was known for going so far as to build huge indoor ponds to float candles in, haul in truckloads of sand, commission renowned visual artists along with new emerging artists, and galvanize hundreds of volunteers for a thirty-hour interactive installation that drew crowds of people from all over the city of Auckland.

It turns out, rather than being powerful and guru-like, Mark was a soft-spoken and humble fellow with a quiet sense of humor and an inviting ability to make the seemingly impossible become quite possible. I could see why volunteers would be drawn to this gentle and insightful curator. He understood the value of each contributor, many kinds of gifts, and the power of community when engaged in a common purpose. The Holy Week installations he led built strong community in his unusual Baptist church and led people from around the large city into an experience like no other.

Sue Wallace, curator of Visions in York, UK, since 1991, describes the long-standing alternative worship community Visions:

> We practice . . . Christian spirituality that mixes ancient and future, prayer and technology, a vibrant multi-sensory experience and creativity. We are part of a movement rather loosely termed Alternative Worship, but the name doesn't really say enough—we mean that our response to the Trinity (God in community) has to be born from our own experience together, as individuals and as a community, and not simply accepting whatever forms of worship are given to us.

However, that is not to say we reject the past, rather that we see Christian traditions as a rich field of possible resource to draw on. But we also draw on contemporary culture in finding expression for our spirituality.[20]

Visions describes themselves as an alt-worship community for people who don't like church and who are reimagining worship. They provide ways to meet through the month in various locations around the city. The rhythms of Visions include three ways of gathering. All gatherings are wide open to anyone. They host "Transcendence," a techno-liturgical high mass with processions, robes, and incense with hip-hop chants and video loop in the mix on the first and third Saturdays of the month. At 4:00 on the fourth Saturday they create a kid-friendly, hands-on gathering for young and older together. This gathering includes songs, crafts, and multimedia experience, and concludes with the ritual of sharing cake. On the evening of the fourth Sunday, their "Low Visions" is held. Low Visions is aptly named for the setup: beanbag chairs and pillows around a large, round, low table, and "blissful video and chill dance beats" by candlelight set the mood. The atmosphere is warm and intimate while holding a sense of mystery and reverence. Bread and wine are shared, and prayers, readings, and reflections are offered throughout the evening. Meaningful personal connections are made here, which often then spill over into community action and formation of real relationships.

These are not formulas to follow but illustrations of what has worked in particular times and places. Creative "don't just sit and listen or follow along" gatherings can take many different forms. Whether you haul truckloads of sand into a building or simply stand in a circle to sing an old-timey hymn, let the unique variety serve as inspiration. Consider how you can incorporate hands-on participation, experiential touch/taste/feel comfort, and a spirit of welcome as you worship in your own place in this very time.

» Questions and Action «

1. Tierra Nueva knows that something special takes place when people from the mainstream and people from the margins study Scripture together. Who might offer a different viewpoint and perspective of Scripture that you can learn from?
2. Who would be at your Beit Midrash if you held one?
3. Are you more comfortable asking questions or being told answers? Why?
4. What resources are available to you for learning? Perhaps a lecture visit from a seminary or university professor, a podcast or teaching video, a good book list and a group of people to read with, or live chats with people who have expertise in a certain area? List the resources you could use.
5. Which worship settings described in this chapter appeal most to you? Why?
6. If the variety of experiences recounted in this chapter can count as worship, what other practices, when shared with others, could you imagine as expressions of worship?

ALT-SUNDAY SCHOOL AND ALT-YOUTH GROUP

Spiritual Formation for Generations to Come

The spiritual formation of children matters. Our children are our future, whether they are children in our own family, in our faith community, or in our neighborhood. Many of us grew up with the tradition of Sunday school and youth group attendance as the best method for teaching children about God. We all knew that good parents sent their children to Sunday school and good children went to Sunday school. The church is also the place where baby dedications and baptisms take place, depending on the denomination and tradition.

What on earth are non-goers to do without Sunday school, youth groups, and baby dedications? This chapter takes a look at what we hope for from Sunday school and youth groups and how we might achieve these objectives without a program and church structure to provide the options.

Let the Little Children: Alt–Sunday School

Remember my friend Teresa's good question, "What do I tell my grandchildren?" Her question tends to be one of the more weighty and worrisome ones for non-goers. It's a tough time to grow up, and as parents we want our kids to have a good spiritual foundation and positive peer groups. We hope they will establish a strong faith and have a real relationship with Christ.

It might surprise you to learn that in the scheme of history, Sunday school is a relatively new addition to church life. Families passed faith from generation to generation prior to the advent of Sunday school. Over the last century people have come to depend on Sunday school as the primary means for spiritual formation of children. It is where kids are expected to become familiar with the stories of the Bible and learn about Jesus. Sunday school lessons today generally convey a simple moral lesson from a Bible story to the children and reinforce that with a craft and songs.

I admit that as a non-goer community leader and now a grandparent, I am a little nervous about this unexplored territory too. What I do know and what brings me comfort to think of is that the Jewish community in Diaspora managed to hold their story and history tight through storytelling and ritual around the family table and prominent celebration of feasts and festivals throughout the year. The repetition of these rites and rituals in the context of relationship and family sunk deep into growing children. I also know that I really disliked Sunday school and youth group as a child and a young person. I learned more sitting with my parents in church or doing my own thinking and reading.

Spiritual formation of children doesn't need to be hard and doesn't need to replicate Sunday school. I believe that children can grasp more than you might expect. I also believe strongly in the power of metaphor and story and hands-on learning (think Leonard Sweet's EPIC). Kids may not be interested in a dry lecture prepared for a patient adult listener (although sometimes you might be surprised by what a child will pick up this way too), but there is no need to dumb down the message or material for them. My Urban Abbey community of non-goers is blessed by the voices, questions, interruptions, prayers, and joy of children. They are free to join in practices with us; the older kids will sometimes join in for communion. They help light prayer candles, share their consolations and desolations over the dinner meal, and some help read Scripture passages at times. Hearing stories, touching bread, dipping into the communion cup, lighting candles—all of these bring children, and adults, into a tangible experience together.

Last month our seven-year-old grandson, Gabriel, not often able to be with us on Sunday evenings, was present at the Urban Abbey gathering for communion. He and his eight-year-old friend, Maya, shared a printed sheet and read a brief liturgy along with the circle of Urban Abbeyites as we prepared for the Eucharist. I could see him reading the words carefully. When we were done with communion, he approached Paul (who'd led communion that evening) and asked, "Could I take this paper home? I want to read it." Paul looked surprised and pleased and told him, "Of course!" Gabe immediately folded it into an intricate paper airplane and tucked it into his pocket.

When we got home he pulled it out and flew it across his room to be read at bedtime. When it came time to tuck Gabe in, he carefully unfolded that airplane liturgy and together we read the words and talked about the meaning. That conversation drew me more deeply into the liturgy and the significance of our Eucharistic gathering. Although I cannot give you formulas or guarantee outcomes, I can encourage you that when you begin to explore how to best engage in the delightful process of the spiritual formation of your own children, you too will be formed.

Non-goers Nate and Candi parent two bright children, Evie and Boaz. Nate and Candi are both natural and intentional in their approach to the spiritual formation of their children. In passing conversation they share what their own experience with God has been and is on a regular basis. The practice of generous hospitality is a consistent faith expression for this family. Although their home is small and was in the middle of a remodel at the time, they welcomed a homeless couple to become part of their household. It was a positive experience that changed all of them. Evie and Boaz know what their mom and dad value and they get to be part of it.

Understanding and respecting the difference in personality of their two children and how they encounter God is also a strong value for Nate and Candi. Candi explained:

> Evie likes emotional conversation about who God is. She likes to pray with us over dinner. Boaz deplores outward shows of emotion, so prayer is uncomfortable for him. He prefers to have cuddle time at night where he asks questions he's been pondering. We have taught them that they don't have to participate in other people's practices, but they should be respectful. So, Boaz doesn't have to bow his head or close his eyes when Evie prays, but he can show her love by being still and quiet while she interacts with God.

Candi wrote readings and prayers for her family to incorporate into family traditions and celebrations. The kids look forward to Mom's liturgy and to lighting candles during family prayer. The whole family loves regularly reading the story of Jesus as told in *The Jesus Storybook Bible*. Candi told me, "I tear up when I am reading it to them. It paints such a picture of love and grace." Evie and Boaz are experiencing faith and formation through conversation, lifestyle, generosity, respect, good story, and the faithfulness of their parents.

When our daughter Kate was in the fifth grade, I designed and taught a weekly class for fourth and fifth graders. The group was made up of six lively boys and Kate. I wanted her to have an experience that engaged her, and I knew I needed to find a way to also draw in the energetic pack of grade school boys.

I informed the parents of my students that their child would have a weekly assignment and a responsibility to bring something specific to help with the lesson each week and that it would be important for a parent to interact and discuss what they'd done in class. I wanted to help these kids gain a good sense of the historical story they are part of and to spark their curiosity and sense of belonging in the story. I wanted them to grow comfortable with Scripture and bring it alive with them. My friend Michele agreed to alternate weeks with me, and we jumped in for one of the most memorable spiritual formation experiences ever.

With all these things in mind, this is how we proceeded: I decided we would let the feasts and festivals of the Old Testament and of Hebrew tradition shape our experience. Using a wide variety of resources, including a Christian resource called *Celebrating Biblical Feasts in Your Home or Your Church* and my favorite, a Reformed Jewish book, *The Jewish Holidays* by Michael Stassfeld, we set out on our learning adventure. We went through the year marking a feast, a festival, a season, or a celebration each Sunday. We built sukkots (small huts) with lumber and vines and twigs and branches in our classroom at harvesttime. We decked them out with hanging fruit and symbols of plenty. We prayed the harvest prayers from Scripture together. We borrowed a shofar (ram's horn) and blew it loud and raspy while we danced the dance of the festival of the New Moon and prayed the prayers and read the Scripture passages that were appropriate for this celebration. We ate feasts of pomegranate, flatbread, goat, and dates, and we reenacted the Esther story at Purim with the dramatic costumes, humor, and all the drama that story deserves. Michele asked a friend who was a practicing Jew to lead us in Seder supper and explain the elements through her eyes and experience.

Every week we together retold our stories from the previous week, practicing God's constant reminder to God's people to always remember. We laughed and were silly and we truly did remember everything. The kids would bring materials each week—nails and grapevines, juice and flatbread, their mother's bathrobe for the costume closet. Nearly every week one of them would call me midweek and ask, "What are we going to do this Sunday? What should I bring!?" I'd hear from their parents how excited they were to tell what they were doing and learning. Their imaginations had been captured in the same way that the Hebrew people had their hearts and minds captured by repetition, story, and hands-on engagement.

I also led the little class in a multisensory process to become familiar with the Nicene Creed. Every week we'd use colored markers and one piece of paper each to slowly write and learn (not memorize—although by the time it was learned it was thoroughly imbedded in us) one small portion of the creed at a time. Week one: "I believe." Week two: "in one God." And so we went. And it did take nearly a year to get to the end.

We'd use as much creativity as we could to artistically customize each of our creed segments and then post them on the wall, ready to add another the following week. While we drew and colored, we'd talk about the significance of those few words and how they connected meaningfully to the words we'd written in previous weeks. Every week we'd read what we'd created and each week there was more to read. At the end of the year these kids proudly spoke the creed with confidence and assurance. Occasionally I run into one of the now young men from the classroom and they bring up the year when we lived out the story of Scripture. One of these times I would like to go through a year of feasts and festivals with adults and children together. Adults could stand to be more playful, and kids don't really need to be taught propositional truths. They need a way of life and a community of belonging.

Infant and Child Baptism and Baby Dedications

My living room has been blessed by any number of significant life rituals. Baby Will Bryan had to be woken from his nap in the bedroom down the hall when he overslept on the afternoon of his baby dedication. His dad gathered the sleepy bundle and quietly carried him to the center of the room, where a circle of friends gently placed their hands on him and on his parents' shoulders to offer prayers of blessing on Will's life. We closed with a simple liturgy read together and then tucked Will back in our crib to resume his nap. Now five years later, Will is an important part of my Urban Abbey community. He is curious, bright, expressive, and is being spiritually formed outside the structure of an institutional church.

Although I was confirmed in the Lutheran church, where infants are traditionally baptized, I was dunked in a baptismal tank in an evangelical church after making a verbal confession of faith when I was in the fourth grade. Infant baptism tends to be something of a mystery to "adult baptism by immersion" folks. My friend Dan, a Lutheran pastor, often finds himself describing the meaning and significance of infant baptism to curious or sometimes suspicious evangelicals. This is not the tradition of my childhood, but it is one I have come to respect. I asked Dan to share a few words on this:

> Convictions about infant baptism vary across Christendom. For me, it is rooted in the grace and promise of God. Through the baptismal waters and God's Word, a seed of faith is planted in the child. As the child grows, that seed is watered and nourished by the Word, the family, and the community. The community models faith for the child, and the child models faith for the community (Luke 18:15–17).

It's possible to see the importance of belonging from the start and coming into the stories and traditions already secure in the knowledge that this is one's community. Little ones are welcomed into the family of God that will hold them for always. I am intrigued by the possibilities for non-goers to create a sense of belonging and place for their young children growing up without the institution of church.

Once a child is old enough to follow simple instructions and hold still for a period of time, they are old enough to join you to help others. Kids can serve, learn, and be formed as they help you weed a neighbor's yard, serve food in a soup kitchen, prepare a meal for a shut-in, and raise money for someone in need. Choose giving opportunities that your children can participate in. Help identify ways they can learn about others and expand their view of the world they live in. Developing a compassionate heart is an important part of spiritual formation.

Creating gatherings that are fun for large groups—adults and kids together—reinforces the message that kids matter. The Beer and Hymns worship gathering is a great example of a good-spirited, kid-*welcoming* (much more than just "kid-friendly") event. There are snack and beverage options for all ages and preferences. The room where Bridge PDX Beer and Hymns meets is easily mopped up and just fine for running (or spilling), and it adjoins an indoor basketball and sports court so children (and adults) can see each other and move from one room to the other, whether they are playing ball or singing with gusto. Hand percussion instruments are strewn on the floor near the musicians, and children are encouraged to come on up and participate in making music. The message to kids is clear: Join in. We want you here.

Our family includes reading the stories of St. Valentine and St. Patrick—both hearty stories of heroes of the faith who lived in remarkable ways—as part of our family tradition on these days. We dine on red food and exchange love notes between family members and remember St. Valentine. On St. Paddy's day we enjoy corned beef with cabbage, carrots, red potatoes, and rye bread along with a good Irish stout, while we revisit the remarkable story of Patrick. Remembering the tales of people of faith who have gone before us connects us all to the greater story.

It isn't as simple as dropping your child off at a Sunday school classroom for sure, but there is a way forward for the spiritual formation of children without the church program of Sunday school. Finding every opportunity for hands-on participation and engaging with Bible stories and stories of people in the history of the church in memorable ways make the Christian story come alive. Kids are formed when we teach practical life skills as spiritual practice and remember to respect their intelligence and capacity. Welcoming kids as important participants in feasts, sacraments, and celebrations will create meaningful and fun family and community traditions that hold the possibility of sticking with them for a lifetime.

Alt–Youth Group

Although I admit that I was not a big fan of church youth group or Sunday school, I do have great memories of high school Young Life group. I felt Jesus in the acceptance of the leaders and the heartfelt times of worship around a campfire with a group of teens. I enjoyed the silly competitions and games and getting to know kids I might not have known otherwise. Having raised three teens, I know that opportunities for peer contact and wild play are important. Teens benefit by opportunities to receive age-specific information. They need peer contact, and they do need recreational outlets.

I know of many instances when parents who were miserable in a church and were ready to become non-goers chose to stay in church because they wanted a youth group for their teenagers. Depending on the circumstance, that might make sense. Those four years of high school go by quickly, and uprooting kids from a peer group they are established in can be traumatizing. On the other hand, I've known of parents who really weren't able to bear staying that full four years and made the decision to leave but encouraged their child to feel free to stay connected to the youth group. And, in these cases, their kids did stay. They stayed, owning their choice and considering the church their own.

Suppose you don't yet have teens or you are wondering if the youth group your teen is in is benefiting your child. Maybe you have teens and feel guilty that you do not attend a church with a big youth group. In spite of the supposition that Christian teens need to be in a youth group, it may be helpful to consider that isolating groups of teenagers in entertainment-based youth groups might not always have the outcome of spiritual formation and long-lasting faith that we hope for.

So, what's a non-goer parent to do? Teenagers are on the verge of adulthood. They need guidance and, at the same time, they need to know that they are taken seriously. When an adult makes the effort to seek out my son and ask him good questions, my son knows that person is genuinely interested in him, and he responds. High school kids are ready to be taught how to listen for ways to join in God's call and to know that they have a greater purpose in this world other than simply pleasing themselves. Teens don't want to be bored, but they do want to be part of something that matters.

I love the perspective of Mark Yaconelli, program director for the Center for Engaged Compassion at Claremont Lincoln University in California. Mark worked with youth for over twenty years and shared these thoughts in an August 1, 2013, blog post:

> Youth long for experience. They long to *do* something . . . "Give me someone to kiss. Give me a road to walk. Give me ashes to grieve. Help me make my own regrets." This kind of raw desire is troubling to parents and manipulated by advertisers, and yet it's exactly this honest ache for life and relationship that Christian communities should cultivate and address . . . They are looking for people willing to struggle for freedom and healing; people willing to risk new forms

of living that resist the frantic, isolating, and violent culture that surrounds us . . . What my children want from religious communities are opportunities for the direct exploration of real living. They don't want to talk about God, they want to live God. They don't want to hear about great deeds, they want to be asked to do great deeds. . . . It is in that pursuit that God is discovered.

Yaconelli went on to share an example of the powerful potential for engaging the passion and intention of young people. This group was comprised of teens from the local high school, not from a church group. They gathered because of relationship.

Overwhelmed with worry and sadness following the 2010 earthquake in Haiti, a group of local adults invited eight Haitian middle and high school students (as well as other interested students) to spend a weekend exploring a Christian approach to suffering. Thirty students signed up. For two days we experimented with various practices that heal suffering (silence, prayer, singing, art, storytelling, solitude). The final night the kids held a prayer vigil that lasted into the wee hours of the morning.[1]

For teenagers, as is true for any of us, real spiritual formation comes from real-life experience. A combination of real experience with a good support system of caring adults may not sound like the typical approach to youth "ministry," but it may make sense for non-goers. Making room for young people to develop leadership gifts and to help shape some aspect of community life can be empowering. Perhaps youth could help with community meal planning or write a liturgy.

I have taken five teenagers to Rwanda with me in the last three years. I guarantee that young people, given the opportunity to connect with others, are some of the best cross-cultural representatives ever. When my daughter Emilie was sixteen, she traveled to northern Somalia (Somaliland) with family friends who were health workers in the capital city of Hargeisa. She spent six weeks helping to deliver babies, feeding and caring for vulnerable newborns, cleaning and holding in a toddler orphanage overflowing with little ones. She still thinks of those six weeks as one of the best times in her life. Well-designed, short-term mission and learning trips and participation in local service opportunities empower teens and remind them that they are part of something larger than themselves.

Helping a teen build his or her own mentoring constellation at this stage in life could be one significant tool for spiritual formation and for equipping them to eventually engage with real-life questions on their own. Parents are strong influences in the lives of their children, but having other adults offer their guidance and encouragement can be a big help. Giving young people permission to ask questions and seek is of real value. Longtime youth group leader now theologian Tony Jones shares from his experience with high school students:

> The questions of faith are among the most vexing existential questions that human beings ask. And the church has done a great disservice to young people by using monological, didactic teaching methods to impart the faith. Adolescents are inherently question-askers. We inhibit their faith development when we conclusively answer their questions, rather than walking with them into deeper questions. In fact, it's obvious to me that the reason the church has lost virtually the entire generation of Millennials is that we gave them high school answers, and when they got to college, those high school answers were no longer sufficient. So they bailed. Instead, we should have given them the tools to further investigate the existential questions that are inherent to the life of faith.

We can convey respect to young people when we welcome youth into community and family discussions. You can bet they have an opinion, and we may learn something from them. I invited my teenage son, Elliot, to read through portions of this book manuscript that I thought might be of some interest to him. He ended up offering some superb perspective and editing advice. Later in the week he followed up with me to see if I'd chosen to incorporate any of his recommendations and was pleased to see that I had.

Giving youth an opportunity to learn to work hard is also good formation. A few summers ago Elliot joined an innovative youth outing designed to give kids the opportunity to earn money, learn work skills, and see what the life of an agricultural worker was like. With good adult supervision, the kids worked alongside migrant workers and a farmer on a large garlic farm for a few days. The work was hard, hot, and eye-opening. Working and saving, and practicing stewardship of money, forms a teen to be free to respond to a sense of call and make their way in the world.

Hailey Scandrette shared about one holistic element of spiritual formation in her family life that made me wish I'd been so wise as to teach my own children the same things. She was taught through hands-on experience that how she uses her money is a spiritual practice. She and her two brothers have been responsible to budget all their expenses for a number of years now. They started with an allowance; then were expected to plan for their clothing, entertainment, charitable giving, and savings; and over time income from part-time jobs replaced their allowance. They were responsible to make a budget and report in every month to share how it was going.

Now nineteen, Hailey is thankful for what she learned through this discipline. She writes, "I'm still finding my own path for living simply, and spending my time and money on what matters most, but I find that identifying and attempting to live out my values make me feel stronger as a person and more connected to the world around me."[2] What if we as non-goers included financial stewardship in the spiritual formation of our kids? Our youngest is now seventeen; we've got one year left to give it a shot!

Along with hard work, we must remember the importance of play. Time goes too quickly. Make sure you play together with your teen; before you know it, they'll be launched. Our family enjoys getting into a long game of Risk or Settlers. Some families play Guitar Hero and others take hikes together.

Designing intermittent outings for groups of teens is another possible component of "when there is no youth group" life. Gather teenagers together for a bike tour, or plan a "movies in the park" night, a laser tag evening, or a campout weekend. A healthy, well-lived life includes play as well as service and hard work.

So, what do we tell our grandchildren? We tell them that a life of faith isn't lived only within the walls of a church. We tell them by the way we live and how we relate with others that Christ is in all that we do. We give them opportunities to discover they have a meaningful place in this world. We play, we work, and we make way for other trustworthy adults to have a place in the lives of our children and young people. We tell stories from Scripture and invite them into the stories and the history of which they are a part. We incorporate metaphor, art, and creativity into our lives and our non-goer communities. We provide a warm, welcoming space for kids and invite them to help shape us. Good Sunday schools and good youth groups in churches will continue to leave a positive impression as my Young Life years did, but for non-goers, there are ways forward too. Alt–Sunday school and alt–youth group may not be half bad for raising responsible young people who hold a strong sense of the greater story of which they are a part.

Here Goes . . . without the Container

Non-goers might miss having an established large church for the weekly connection with people who can offer advice, work together to achieve large-scale projects, and provide a one-stop resource base for classes and training. This is, however, a fascinating time in history, full of unprecedented opportunity for non-goers. In a way that never has been possible before, people can connect, network, and make things happen through the Internet, through informal networks, and with the encouragement and support of many others who find themselves identifying with the Wild Goose as non-goers in this world.

May these examples of being Christian—of creative gatherings and faithful curators—serve as reassuring images and of possibility outside of the structure of the traditional church. May these stories lead to transformation for us and for others. Meeting Jesus while studying Scripture with a felon, holding tradition in the respectful spirit of sankofa, and teaching theology under a tree in the backyard; welcoming children and befriending strangers, sharing consolation and desolation over a bowl of soup, and gathering in alt-worship settings; making space for everyone at the table, building wells in Africa via the Internet, and sharing Eucharist on the front porch; tending to each one in our communities, young and old; making simple weddings in living rooms and baptisms in the river; and becoming a priesthood of all believers bearing responsibility for one another . . . these are points of entry and places of nourishment and connection for non-goers that can overflow and bless many.

⊗ Questions and Action ⊗

1. What do you think about kids being contributors and participants alongside adults? What do you like about the concept and what concerns does it raise for you?
2. Whether or not you have children, where and how can you create a "kid-welcoming" environment in your life?
3. What do you think of Jones's suggestion that one reason Millennials are not returning to church is because we've raised them on simple answers? How comfortable or uncomfortable are you with teenagers expressing doubts and asking questions?

12

PARISH IS HIP

Rooted in the Neighborhood for Good

The Word became flesh and blood, and moved into the neighborhood. We saw the glory with our own eyes, the one-of-a-kind glory, like Father, like Son, Generous inside and out, true from start to finish.

John 1:14 Message

What does it look like when that sort of glory, the kind that moves into neighborhoods and is generous inside and out, shows up? A desire to find roots, the strain of the economy, a longing for real connection and community, and the search for ways to engage in lasting change are together stirring people to a new level of commitment and care for their neighborhoods. This chapter tells some of those encouraging stories.

Right Where You Are

As a member of the coordinating group for Portland Parish Collective, I frequently get to hear from and see the work of inspiring, ordinary people who are committed to taking local action and to deep community building for the good of their neighborhood. They take to heart the example of Christ: to move into the neighborhood, to be present and with people. As Christ was God incarnate—fully God and fully human—someone we could see and feel, so we are called to be Christ to people, incarnating and redeeming the places where we live and work, for the good of all. Rooting and settling in a neighborhood to serve and love and learn is one way non-goers are shifting their focus. This awareness is also growing in the institutional church as she shifts with the changing times.

There are plenty of trendy terms to describe this growing shift: missional church or missional living, parish-based ministry (not a new idea but one with resurgence toward vitality), incarnational living, church without walls, slow church, and rootedness. They all point in a similar direction. While they call us to something more than ourselves, they also call us simply to be ourselves, right where we are. Traditionally, a parish is the smallest unit of organization for the Roman Catholic and the Episcopal Church. It can also be understood as a township, village, or neighborhood that has its own church. The wisdom of commitment to place that was embedded in the Roman Catholic Church began to slowly wane with the Reformation. Dr. Ray Bakke explores the result of this historical shift:

> The evangelicalism I grew up with had a theology of persons and programs, but it lacked a conscious theology of place. Protestants generally cut themselves off from "parish" thinking—an ongoing commitment to their place of ministry—so that when a church's location became "inconvenient" it simply relocated to a new place, often near a freeway (reflecting our society's shift from a walking to an automobile culture). Along the way, we abandoned real estate that had been prayed for fervently by Christians before us—and along with it abandoned any commitment to the neighborhoods we left behind.[1]

My friend Pastor Rose Madrid-Swetman leads her congregation into a renewed understanding of the theology of place. She likes to call this missional move "making church big" rather than "making big church." Many churches pursue an attractional model, seeking growth in size and number. Rose has led her little congregation toward small but strategic acts of faithfulness for the benefit of the neighborhood they are situated in. Vineyard Community Church of Shoreline (VCC) is being "church big" with incredible results. The congregation has identified two primary purposes for existing. First, they value the discipline of spiritual practices. It is their connection with God that enables them to serve well. Second, they as a congregation exist to serve the low income suburban community of Shoreline, Washington, where their building is located.

They have built relationships with people from the immigrant community in county housing down the street. Out of those relationships have come after-school tutoring and free parenting and marriage classes. The congregation provides school supplies and haircuts. The county housing residents and VCC communities celebrate together with an annual Festival of Lights party. They started a community garden with neighbors to benefit the neighborhood. VCC is the first church to have become partners with human services in their county to help address the overwhelming variety of needs in this neighborhood.

When they first started getting involved in the neighborhood, their efforts were met with great suspicion by neighbors and county leaders. Now, after demonstrating they really do exist to serve people and not to get something for themselves or to seek conversions, they are sought out for counsel and for help with special projects. Not long ago, the human services director asked Rose why they cared. Rose replied that they were just following Jesus by loving their neighbors. The director, not a Christian herself, replied, "Sounds good to me!" In the three years since the church made an intentional move to missional identity and action, the congregation has grown spiritually and, although it was not a goal, it has grown in size as others are drawn to join in mission in their own neighborhood.

This church is just one example of what can happen when we turn attention from ourselves to the biblical call of God's heart for the needs of the poor and of the neighborhood we are situated in. When we ask our neighbors what they need and want rather than deciding what they need and want, and when we then make time, resources, buildings, homes, and energy available to meet those needs, we are engaging in the mission of the kingdom of God. We are joining in the creative work of healing and redeeming the whole world. To put it simply, whether we are involved in missional community, missional church, or missional lifestyle, when we are willing to pay attention to what God is already doing, and join in to serve others, we grow spiritually and the world changes.

Alan Hirsch, missiologist Michael Frost, and Alan Roxburgh of Forge; Kathy Escobar of The Refuge; Paul Sparks and Tim and Cote Soerens of Parish Collective; and Steve Knight, cofounder and community architect of TransFORM Network are also all leading the way in localized, missional living. This is how Alan Hirsch of Forge puts it: by nature God is a "sent one." God takes the initiative to redeem creation. "This doctrine, known as missio Dei—the sending of God—is causing many to redefine their understanding of the church. . . . A missional theology is not content with mission being church-based work. Rather, it applies to the whole life of every believer."[2] We all are to be agents of the kingdom of God and "carry the mission of God into every sphere of life."[3]

My friend Kathy Escobar has built her ministry on the principle that there is no "them or us—only us." We cannot be "good Christians and go help those poor people who are not like us" and at the same time truly forge friendship with people in our neighborhood.[4] "As we acknowledge our own pain, we cultivate the ability to feel, comfort, and enter into the pain of others. . . . Acknowledging pain helps us tear down the barriers that keep us from relationship and our own humanity."[5]

Getting in touch with our own pain and becoming aware of our own brokenness is not an easy path, but it's one that leads to our own transformation as well as the possibility of forming authentic relationships. No matter how many good intentions we have, if we are not becoming more self-aware and taking active measures to continue toward growth and healing, our work and our relationships can only go so far and may end up causing more harm than good over time. Structures and institutions don't always easily accommodate or support what Kathy often refers to as this "messy way" of being authentic. After years in church leadership, Kathy has come to believe that we may need to "abandon the infrastructure if it means sacrificing people and relationships for the sake of a structure that always needs to be maintained."[6]

Missiologist Lesslie Newbigin calls local congregations to "renounce an introverted concern for their own life, and recognize that they exist for the sake of those who are not members, as sign, instrument, and foretaste of God's redeeming grace for the whole life of society."[7] That sounds fancy, but it means if we can learn to walk with others, in ordinary ways and places, we help bring grace and healing to our neighborhoods and cities—to the whole of society right where we are. I would add that in the process we receive grace and are healed as well. The fact is that we need to start with our own neighborhood, our own zip code, to work toward making a better society and world.

Steve Knight looks at broader society and suggests wisely that "followers of Jesus will need to practice greater humility in approaching people of other faiths and spiritualities (or those who profess no faith at all), and engaging in interfaith dialogue for the sake of understanding and partnership in making the world a better place should become a high missional priority."[8] Escobar emphasizes the importance of humility and personal healing to be missional, and Newbigin calls us to serve others right where we are. Emotional health, sacrificial service, and humble understanding are postures to assume if we want to share the good news of the Christ story.

Neighborhood Living Rooms and Dining Rooms

I stumbled across a blog post by author Shauna Niequist about her friend Sarah Harmeyer from Dallas, Texas, who wanted to find a tangible way to build community.[9] Sarah set a goal to host five hundred new people in her home in 2012. Her handy father built her an awesome outdoor table and benches that could seat twenty-two people, and she set out to create community around that table. My heart leapt when I read Shauna's account of Sarah's open table and her big goal.

Sarah knew the names of only two neighbors when she started out. By the time she reached her goal of meeting and hosting five hundred new people (a whole month before the year ended), she'd come to really, really know fifty neighbors. The gatherings were intergenerational and covered the political and religious spectrum. People came for mini-concerts, soup lunches, and sumptuous dinners. As they came, they became friends with others they would not likely meet otherwise—more neighbors know more neighbors because of Sarah's table.

Sarah had a desire to connect and create community, and her motto was "the more the merrier." She didn't wait for someone to start a program and she didn't knock on doors inviting neighbors to church. She reached out in the embrace of simple but determined hospitality. Every guest signed that well-purposed table with a sharpie and left with a connection they hadn't had before. They felt the welcome. A neighborhood of strangers became a neighborhood of friends because of the intention of one young woman and her big, hospitable table and welcoming spirit. Darrell Guder, in *Missional Church*, says this of hospitable communities of faith: "The practice of Christian hospitality . . . indicates the crossing of boundaries (ethnic origin, economic condition, political orientation, gender status, social experience, educational background) by being open to and welcoming of the other. Without such communities of hospitality, the world will have no way of knowing that all God's creation is meant to live in peace."[10]

Sarah, rooted in the particularity of her zip code and practicing the crossing of boundaries, did indeed help make the world a better place in a particular location. And so can we, right where we are. Church without walls can be rooted and incarnated around a picnic table, a playground, or a garden bed.

You could think of it as waking up to see your neighborhood with new eyes. Ben and Cherie Katt used to think of the Aurora strip in Seattle, Washington, as the part of town you hope you don't have to detour through to get to where you really want to go. Aurora is comprised of abandoned city blocks and is neglected and overlooked in the trendy city of Seattle. Drug trafficking, seedy motels, and the sex industry have been known to thrive in the Aurora area. Along with their two young children and a few dozen young seminary graduates from Seattle School of Theology and Psychology, they decided they would root themselves in this area and get to know the people. This group of young people called themselves Awake Church, and they committed to paying attention to, or being awake to, their neighborhood. That new perspective gave birth to Aurora Commons, a neighborhood living room to the Aurora strip. Since then, things have changed. "After three years of learning from our Aurora neighbors and building community through barbecues in motel parking lots, birthday parties at local parks, gardening, conversations on the 358 metro bus, etc., we felt it was time to create a space together where our lives could intersect more intentionally on a daily basis . . . and so, the Aurora Commons came to be."[11]

Aurora Commons is now home and gathering space for a daily coffee hour, weekly women's breakfasts, children's activities, community dinners, open mic nights, and educational classes in which neighbors share their skills with one another. Aurora Commons is used to host storytelling workshops, where neighbors learn to tell and reflect on their own life stories. Yoga classes, counseling, and massage can be found on-site. Awake partners can be found with their Aurora neighbors who are transitioning from homelessness into housing or seeking emergency shelter. They are collaborating with other local groups to start up a mobile medical clinic. More important than the "doing" are the relationships that have formed and that can inform the "doing." Awake friends take time to sit with and love their neighborhood and neighbors in practical ways. This sort of engagement requires long-term commitment. Deep rootedness makes way for new hope and healing for all, which seems quite fitting in a neighborhood named Aurora—meaning, "new dawn."

The Church of the Savior, referenced in chapter 8, was founded by Gordon and Mary Cosby in Washington, D.C., after World War II, and broke with convention from the start. Their way of being remains an example to others who seek to be the church without walls and to bless the neighborhood in which they are situated. They were emphatic about staying small and committing to action with no spectators allowed. "We've got to move from believing . . . to doing," Cosby declared. "We've got to keep in mind the discrepancy between belief and embodiment."[12] For more than sixty years now, that vision for embodying the life of Christ in the city has been borne out. Members are required to commit to both the inward work of study and prayer and to the outward practice of social justice.

Gordon Cosby's chaplaincy in Europe during the Second World War shaped his views and informed his path forward. He came to believe that "denomination and race were artificial constructs and that people should live in regular life as they would in war—willing to lay down their lives for their neighbors, viewing their faith as an urgent tool to change the world."[13]

A *Washington Post* article reports that "Thousands of people are served by dozens of organizations started by the church, part of the intense social justice work mandatory for members. One of its programs found jobs for 800 people last year. Another provided 325 units of affordable housing." At the time of his retirement in 2009 at age ninety-one, Cosby "noted that megachurches, now struggling to manage their size, have come to the church for guidance on how to be small." He said of mega-churches, "This form is dying, and whatever new form will happen is vague. . . . We are wary of people who say they already know what that will be."[14] Cosby lived to a ripe age of ninety-five. At the time of his death in 2013, he was still keeping an active blog and was engaged in racial reconciliation in small groups. His legacy informs what those future forms of church might be.

Whether it is a church without walls, a missional faith community existing for the sake of others, or determined hospitable individuals with a vision to bring people together for the good of their own zip code, the power of people coming together for good cannot be denied. Gordon and Mary's lifetime of work in their Washington, D.C., neighborhood is a testament to that.

When we stop to listen and learn from our neighbors and neighborhood, the need of the neighborhood itself can inform our action. To do something *with* people rather than *for* people means we need to learn and understand where to go and what to do. Non-goers, motivated by love for neighbor, are applying themselves to the building blocks of neighborhood: park cleanup days, pedestrian safety and walk-able streets, welcoming outdoor gathering spaces, availability of fresh local produce and healthy food, supporting local businesses, public art installations for all to enjoy, and bike repair clinics. Loving our neighborhood can be expressed in so many particular ways. And whether it means installing park benches or collaborating with local government for good water runoff systems, it always begins with listening.

My own city, Portland, Oregon, is chock-full of stories of neighbors caring and taking action to create the kind of neighborhood they want for themselves and others. I love this story from the corner of NE 30th and Killingsworth. Once a dangerous street crossing, it has become a place of neighborhood connection and creativity. Concerned neighbors had long asked the city to step in and create a crosswalk. Finally one neighbor stepped in, and things began to change. Neighbor Asula Press got a $600 grant and invited other local residents to join her in changing the face of the intersection. They began planning and painting and turned a hazardous crossing into a colorful mural. These neighbors naturally slowed traffic with their brilliant street art. The effort brought neighbors together, made their street safer, and got the attention of the city. Between 2007 and 2010 the city added "zebra safety stripes" and eventually a flashing light. Over time neighbors have added large mosaic planter boxes and installed bike corrals. A neighborhood problem has become a neighborhood asset.[15]

These neighbors were exercising what Portland, Oregon-based City Repair calls "organized group action that . . . inspires communities and individuals to creatively transform the places where they live."[16] City Repair builds on the idea of my favorite urban planner, Jane Jacobs, that "localization—of culture, of economy, of decision-making—is a necessary foundation of sustainability."[17]

> By creatively reclaiming urban spaces to create community-oriented places, we plant the seeds for greater neighborhood communication, empower our communities and nurture our local culture. Placemaking is a multi-layered process within which citizens foster active, engaged relationships to the spaces which they inhabit, the landscapes of their lives, and shape those spaces in a way which creates a sense

of communal stewardship and lived connection. As the process of developing a community place proceeds; people develop deeper relationships and more energy to create together because they live together. Creating a common ground that transcends the differences among people powerfully addresses this isolation and creates an environment where people feel like they can do anything they set their collective minds to.[18]

What could happen in our neighborhoods if this was the spirit that animated us—non-goers and goers alike? It isn't a stretch to see the values of Jesus in these efforts. Christ who became like us, Christ who gave his life to heal the world and connect us, Christ who lives in Trinitarian community is present when we come together for a greater good.

Springwater Intentional Community in Southeast Portland is always up to something interesting. Living in several houses on the same block in a strategically selected, worn-down area on the fringes of Portland, this small community of Christians worship together, live simply, work for justice, keep the nearby parkway clean, and make friends with neighbors. One of their recent contributions to the well-being of the neighborhood is coordinating the construction of microlibraries. Although it took longer than if Springwater had built the libraries themselves, they involved other neighbors around them, created real community ownership, and all got to know each other better in the process. Small glass-front cabinets on legs or stands were built and installed around the Lents-Springwater neighborhood where they are situated. Stocked with used books to be borrowed, neighbors can help themselves to a book, add a book to share, keep a book, or read and then return a book for another reader. The inventory self-rotates, people share, and reading is encouraged. This is part of Springwater's gospel calling.

In the same spirit, one Springwater household with a corner lot involved the whole neighborhood in a planning process to build a large and comfortable covered seating area facing the street. This provides a neutral "third space" for neighbors to gather and chat or to sit for a rest as they stroll around the neighborhood.

Heading a little farther north to Washington State and downtown Tacoma, we can find some inspiration with Zoe Livable Church. Zoe started out as an attractional community—a church designed to draw young people from around the city. Pastor and church planter Paul Sparks became dissatisfied as he began to realize that his growing congregation was made up of people mainly coming to "consume" a service. With a small group of other Zoe leaders, a choice was made to shift the purpose of Zoe from a church growth model to a deeply rooted, high-commitment, faith community devoted to serving and being part of the neighborhood they were in. Members were invited to relocate to a twenty-square-block section of downtown Tacoma. As might be expected, the faith community quickly shrunk in size. Instead of investing in planning highly produced, energetic church services, Zoe members now spend their time loving people and creating a better neighborhood.

Several women in the Zoe community have opened and are operating small businesses in areas that had been neglected. This kind of investment is bringing economic vitality and points of neighborhood connection alive. The Zoe community gathers for simple faith practices, now led by wise and soft-spoken Liz Sparks, married to founder Paul Sparks. Zoe member Holly Knoll, in coordination with Tacoma Urban Landscaping, piloted a Yarn Bombers project to promote walking in the neighborhood. Holly and other friends handy with knitting needles literally went to town creating whimsical knit covers for fire hydrants, colorful wraps for stop sign posts, and hundreds and hundreds of bright knit flowers and garlands to fasten festively along previously uninviting stretches of cyclone fencing. The yarn art marked the way for the walk-able neighborhood project, encouraging people to get out on foot and connect with their neighbors.

Sitting at my dining table for conversation over coffee, Paul spoke with admiration and respect for the transformative work that the women of Zoe have brought to bear in the neighborhood.

> In downtown Tacoma, as is the case in many neighborhoods, it's the women who are leading exemplary work that produces flourishing, livable communities. Engagement in micro-entrepreneurship, small business ownership, co-op projects, creation of third places, crime watches, community gardens, hyper-local non-profits, access to and distribution of local food, local environmental care, planning built environments for multi-generational use—really the list goes on. I have to ask myself, what can we learn from this? What are the paradigm shifts, behavioral and mindset changes that need to take place to bring life to neighborhoods everywhere? Empower the women, follow them and listen to them. See what sort of transformation they lead.[19]

Paul has learned from his "wake-up" experience as an earnest young church planter. He's learned as his vision has changed and as he's let go of control and aspirations for a certain kind of success. That learning coalesced into the formation of the Parish Collective in partnership with bright, young, parish-based leaders Tim and Cote Soerens. Parish Collective serves to find and tell the stories of locally rooted communities, motivated by faith and the love of neighbor to encourage Christians to a resurgence of local commitment. Inhabit, the annual Parish Collective gathering, hosted by the Seattle School of Theology and Psychology, has become a pilgrimage for people pioneering in local connection and rootedness, providing a venue for those stories to be told and shared. Even more important, Parish Collective and Inhabit provide an opportunity for parish leaders to meet. This intention is captured in the Parish Collective tagline, "Rooted and Linked." To this end, the Seattle School of Theology and Psychology and Parish Collective have joined forces for a ministry certificate program called Leadership in the New Parish to gather parish-minded Christians and equip them for what is ahead. When we are not isolated we can learn from the mistakes of others, share new ideas, celebrate victories, and get fresh perspective.

My imagination is also captured by the possibilities of something called "cash mobs." You may have heard of "flash mobs"—groups of people who gather in a certain location and break into energetic song and dance routines to the surprise and delight of bystanders. Cash mobs don't necessarily sing, but instead they congregate with intention in a fun-spirited spending spree to support locally owned businesses. Engineer Chris Smith came up with the cash mob concept. He describes them as "sort of a reverse Groupon. Instead of offering people bargain-basement deals, people pay the regular price to support retailers in their communities."[20]

Here's how his idea works: cash mobbers commit to spending at least $20 at the mobbed business of the day. Social media—such as Facebook and Twitter—is used in advance to nominate and select the business to be mobbed. The business is informed before mob day so they can be sure to have extra customer service on hand. On the shopping day selected, people mob the store with their money in hand, ready to buy.

For small businesses with limited advertising budgets, struggling to compete with big box stores, this provides exposure and—cash. Shoppers are reminded that local businesses really matter and are encouraged to forge relationships with their local retailers. Non-goers can make a difference and have fun sponsoring a cash mob. Taking responsibility to see to the survival of small businesses in our neighborhoods brings life and hope to an area. Shopping can be a practice of geographically based ecclesiology. Forming communities that wake up to this kind of renewal and practical application of loving one's neighbor is a mission that is just the right size. Christ, who made himself local and rooted himself in a particular place at a particular time in history, invites us to engage in local solutions and connection for the good of the world.

When learning from our neighborhoods, taking small steps, engaging in practical action, and building relationships right where we are, Kathy Escobar's wise counsel reminds our self-obsessed culture that we really exist for the sake of others. At the same time, if we blindly run out to be do-gooders without, at some level, first acknowledging our own need, broken places, personal pain, and shortsightedness, we are going to end up creating a new trail of pain and finding ourselves unable to have genuine friendship with our neighbors. We don't need to be whole, but we do need to be humble. We flat out aren't perfect, so we might as well be keenly aware of that. We might be more likely to be wrong than right, so becoming a learner is essential. This need not stop us from jumping in; it should, however, inform our way of being and our action.

As non-goers we are well advised to follow Gordon and Mary Cosby's ideal for the people of God—fully embrace spiritual formation and personal growth, and at the same time, pair that with real, vigorous, humble, nitty-gritty social action. Then spread out and scatter to form small communities of practical change and transformation.

Whether we are choosing how and where to spend our money, thinking about safe streets and intersections, creating beauty to inspire and to connect people, teaching kids to swim or read, inviting people to write on our dining tables with sharpies, or creating little libraries and shared spaces with our neighbors, we must first wake up to our own need and then to the need and hope of the neighborhood. When we do so, we are speaking to the deep human hunger for connection, and we become part of this amazing story of bringing the good news of the redemption of all things—right where we are.

Questions and Action

1. Bakke talked about having a theology of place. A theology of place asks, "Who are your neighbors?" Do you know who your neighbors are?
2. What would it look like to carry the mission of God into your neighborhood?
3. Cosby's community allowed "no spectators" and insisted on moving from "believing to action." How could living with these values change you?

13

INTENTIONAL COMMUNITIES

Constructing a Life Together

"The restoration of the church will surely come from a sort of new monasticism which has in common with the old only the uncompromising attitude of a life lived according to the Sermon on the Mount in the following of Christ. I believe it is now time to call people together to do this."[1]

Although these words were written by Dietrich Bonhoeffer in 1935, they speak powerfully to a growing movement of young and not-so-young people who are committing themselves to be the church in a new/old way. What is taking place may or may not look like Bonhoeffer imagined, but something is taking shape and spreading as Christians far and wide come together in a variety of small communities committed to "a life lived" in simplicity, humility, and for others. As cofounder of the intentional community Urban Abbey in North Portland, I know the benefit of learning from the stories of others. The following pages tell stories of a variety of innovative, neo-monastic communities making a real difference today.

While you may or may not wish to or choose to take the leap into something as disruptive as joining or forming an intentional community, the stories in this chapter contain inspiring and doable ideas that you can try out in your own life and neighborhood no matter what. We aren't called to all be the same, but we are called to grow and give. Read with that in mind and see what is sparked in your own imagination.

Neo What?

Historically, monastic orders have formed as renewal movements or responses to excess or neglect of the poor or to political co-option in the church. The Simple Way, Rutba House, Reba Place, Church of the Sojourner, Little Flowers Community, Church of the Servant King, Communality, JPUSA, and Mustard Seed House—along with hundreds of other less visible communities—are leading the way reviving the age old tradition of monastic Christian communities and looking to live out the essentials of faith in day-to-day life.

Some refer to themselves as neo-monastic community; others call themselves intentional community. All participate in some form of shared life, rituals, and spiritual practices. Some communities share housing; in others, members live in close geographic proximity in a particular neighborhood. Values for peacemaking, reconciliation, spiritual formation, shared resources, hospitality to strangers, service to the poor, and stewardship of the earth are commonly held. Often these communities are strategically located in poor neighborhoods, and they work to befriend, serve, and learn from their neighbors. The Simple Way founder Shane Claiborne and Jonathan Wilson-Hartgrove of Rutba House have become well-known, compelling, prophetic voices from this expression.

A few years ago Shane Claiborne, with his marvelous messy dreadlocks, floppy homemade clothing, and relaxed Southern twang, visited George Fox University in Newberg, Oregon. Shane had an attentive audience of college students on the edges of their seats as he drew them into stories of possibility and hope from his neighborhood. After this presentation I had the chance to sit with Shane and trade stories—of the beauty and challenge of the Simple Way community life, of an Urban Abbey dream in process, and of this matter of being a Christian without going to church.

The Simple Way is a community situated in one of the nation's poorest neighborhoods, Kensington, Philadelphia, which has been racked with joblessness and is known for its vacant homes and factories. They aim to "plot goodness" in the form of practical projects and relationship with their neighbors. Shane explains: "To live in loving relationships with each other, we know that we need to be people of prayer. Learn to pray together. Prayer is not an excuse for inaction. John Perkins likes to say, 'You are God's hands and feet: get out there.'"

I asked Shane to tell me more about what "getting out there" looked like for the Simple Way. "It means when we ask God to move a mountain, we need to be ready for God to hand us a shovel. For some strange reason, God does not want to change the world without us. As we pray, we prepare ourselves to act and to become the change we want to see. It can be hard to believe that you have a beautiful Creator if a lot of what you see is ugly.

"Caring about where our food comes from and what our neighbors eat and growing beautiful gardens is good news—it makes the gospel visible. And that is what we mean by incarnation—'in flesh'—love with skin. The Catholics have taught me a lot through the Eucharist—you are what you eat. The mystery of being the body of Christ is that we join the incarnation, the manifestation of God's love in the world. Hospitality is an important part of community life. To be people of reconciliation, racial and economic, it needs to first happen at our tables and in our homes. Church happens around dinner tables and in our living rooms."

Another development that was bringing joy was the many ways that people were coming to the community to use their gifts. Shane gave the example of actors who produced a collaborative art camp for kids in the neighborhood, a scientist who was working on area projects to make sure the neighbors would be able to drink reliable, safe, clean water, and a carpenter who was giving his time to rebuild abandoned houses. He grinned broadly as he said, "The call to radical discipleship is not a call to sameness. Unity doesn't mean uniformity."

When asked for advice and guidance for people who are thinking of forming monastic community, Shane said, "Use your imagination to practice resurrection in tough neighborhoods. Dorothy Day talked of the importance of being intentional about creating environments that make it easier to be good." ("I cannot stress this enough—we must never forget our objective and that is to 'build that kind of society where it is easier for people to be good.' This is what Peter Maurin taught us."[2])

Shane also mused about how intentional communities can help shape people in vocation. "Help people discover what it means to use their skills and vocation missionally right where they are. What would it mean to be a missional robotics engineer? They might build robots to disarm land mines. What would happen to a young law student who spent a year immersed in urban life? They might still become a lawyer, but they will be a different kind of lawyer. When our passions meet the world's pain, that is, when we find our purpose and vocation—that's where the magic happens."

"What would you say to people reading this book, people who might be asking, can I be a Christian and not go to church?" I asked Shane. He nodded and replied with a slight smile, "The early Christians said that we cannot have God as our Father if we don't accept the church as our mother. But we can also see that our mother is in need of healing. Being a Christian is an invitation to join an organism, not just an organization—we are now a part of the Body of Christ alive in the world."

He added that we have to "stop complaining about the church that we've experienced and start becoming the church that we dream of. Be careful about saying we are going to do it better than anyone before. Shifts and changes in the church are nothing new. Jesus is not scared to see people walk away. Every few hundred years it seems this is something that happens; people rethink what it means to be Christian. Good changes have come from the desert and the margins in the past—the Desert Fathers and Mothers, St. Francis and St. Clare. We are figuring out what it means to be the church now." Shane leaned forward in his chair as he added this word to non-goers: "Ask questions: Is God's dream the same as Wall Street's dream? Will good change come through culturally relevant, creative worship services that draw a crowd? Maybe not. Early Christianity was a way of life. The Way. When we live in ways that resemble Jesus, then we are the fragrance of Christ in the world." This is indeed the beautiful invitation. What might happen if non-goers everywhere said yes to it?

Ancient-Future Communities

The following quote from second-century philosopher Aristides brings me up short every time I read it or hear it. It is true that the power of lives well lived in the way of love and for the benefit of others is truly magnetic.

> It is the Christians, O Emperor, who have sought and found the truth, for they acknowledge God. They do not keep for themselves the goods entrusted to them. They do not covet what belongs to others. They show love to their neighbours. They do not do to another what they would not wish to have done to themselves. They speak gently to those who oppress them, and in this way they make them their friends. It has become their passion to do good to their enemies. They live in the awareness of their smallness. Anyone of them who has anything gives ungrudgingly to the one who has nothing. If they see a travelling stranger, they bring him under their

roof. They rejoice over him as a real brother, for they do not call one another brothers out of the flesh, but they know that they are brothers in the spirit and in God. If they hear that one of them is imprisoned or oppressed for the sake of Christ, they take care of all his needs. If possible, they set him free. If anyone among them is poor or comes into want while they themselves have nothing to spare, they fast two or three days for him. In this way they can supply any poor man with the food he needs. This O Emperor, is the rule of life of the Christians, and this is their manner of life.[3]

The web directory of the Fellowship for Intentional Community lists 218 neo-monastic and intentional communities. I am personally aware of dozens and dozens not represented on that site. The impulse that guides these 218 plus communities, Simple Way, and Springwater is nothing new. Throughout the centuries, social realities and concerns have prompted Protestant and Roman Catholic Christians to form communities that helped them to live in what they felt was the way of Jesus for the good of the world. Some of these communities have come and gone, and others have grown or held steady over time.

Steve Collins offers a helpful survey of various flavors and purposes of intentional communities. He identifies communities that are formed with an emphasis on spiritual formation and discipling. Some communities live according to what is called a rule, an "explicit declaration of values and practices" that shape the day-to-day life of the community. Some communities form for the purpose of supporting countercultural ways of living. Others are "prophetic communities—public demonstration of alternative values and possibilities." Many communities have a missional focus, reaching out and taking action in the world. He makes the important distinction that "neo-monastic groups emphasize community built around a rhythm of shared spiritual practices, rather than creative worship events."

Each of these community purposes can be a valid reason to exist. Intentional or neo-monastic community will form and function with a greater emphasis on one of these values more than others and some will incorporate all or most of the values. In all cases we can learn something from our sisters and brothers who are taking this path.[4]

Big House and Friendship

Sipping a cup of freshly brewed tea at Townshend's Tea Company on NE Alberta in Portland, I enjoyed conversation with Maria, an engaging high school instructor and intentional community leader. Maria is Roman Catholic and comes to intentional community by tradition. In the 1970s her parents formed a strong intentional community called Big House. Her experience growing up in such a strong community stuck with her, and after she married, Maria, along with friends, established Friendship Community in Northeast Portland. In addition to day-to-day life in Friendship, she and her family participate in gatherings at the Big House community, which continues on to this day.

I was intrigued to hear more about life in Big House, a community that had so captured the heart of this second generation member that she'd chosen a similar way of life for her own family. Maria explained that Big House was a house of hospitality from 1972 to 2012, for forty years! It was started by three couples and one single person, and included five children. Since 1978 the community has been made up of five families (including two of the original families) living in the same, older North Portland neighborhood where the Big House is situated. The community also includes weekly women's and men's groups of about fifteen people each. The neighborhood extension of Big House is referred to as the Five Family community.

Maria continued, "My parents still live in the original Big House. They continued to provide hospitality until eighteen months ago. Even though their health does not allow for them to extend full-time hospitality now, they do have a gentleman who provides spiritual direction from their home. They continue with their faith-prayer group of many years; they also continue to lead a theology book group." She explained that even now many projects and events come from Big House and the Five Family community. "The original purpose of Big House was at least twofold: conservation of resources and hospitality along with a strong source of support and challenge for our countercultural values, such as anticonsumerism, intentional and careful media consumption, hospitality, and relationships as a priority over other measures of success."

When Big House first formed, they had a vision for providing transitional support and a home to men recently paroled. Maria shared that after living with the community for several months, one of their household members on parole robbed them. Maria's parents had provided transitional housing to other parolees prior to the formation of the community, so this event may not have put them off, but other community members decided they preferred to shift the ministry to providing housing for teens, women, and children escaping abuse and to serve as a resource for other people who came to their parish, St. Andrew Catholic Church, seeking housing.

Reflecting on childhood memories of life in Big House, Maria told me, "We had dinner together every night. You can imagine how seven adults and five children plus our guests made for a lively dinner time. The community was shaped by everyone who lived there. While the values of simplicity and hospitality were constant, what we ate, how we prayed, what activities we did, changed with who was sharing the table. One woman named Mary, who prior to living with us existed in extreme poverty and homelessness, would make graham crackers with cheddar cheese and peas on her cook night. As young teenagers, my sister and I didn't enjoy her dinners, but we understood that her previously limited resources had limited her cooking repertoire. The parolees were noteworthy to us as children for their lack of independence;

they asked to go to the bathroom, to go outside, to use the stove." These relationships gave Maria and her sister unique insight into the greater world and a diverse group of friends. By her thirteenth birthday in November 1978, nearly eighty people had lived in Big House with them. "I know because for that birthday I asked if we could invite everyone who'd ever lived with us to come celebrate."

She described the long-term commitment of community members to each other to be like an "extended chosen family. We are three generations now. My father is the oldest at seventy-five and the youngest are infants. I'm the oldest of the second generation at forty-seven. We still celebrate Passover Seder, Bastille Day, All Saints/All Souls, Advent, and Epiphany together every year, from 1978 to the present."

I asked Maria about her own community, Friendship Community. She explained, "We were gathered by a friend who participated in the Jesuit Volunteer Corps after college, which is true of most of us. Whenever a house went up for sale within a three-block radius of 29th and Alberta, he would call, cajole, invite, and encourage one of us to buy it. Nine couples/families moved in between 1995 and 1998. We formed on the basis of shared values, simplicity, and social justice. Some were part of a shared religious community, St. Andrew, and others were not church-goers. Our name is Friendship Community, as we go beyond the normal parameters of friendship to support one another. Six families remain together, although three households are now farther to the east in Portland. There are also more than a handful of other families who participate in some of our activities."

She described what the life of Friendship looks like. "We have a one-room cottage in our backyard for our women's and men's groups. We provide assistance to one another and our extended families and co-workers, we visit each other's elderly parents, bring meals to those with newborns or injuries, raise money for justice causes and charities, attend antiwar demonstrations together, and teach and tutor one another's children. We also share resources: carpooling for school, lawn mowers, outdoor furniture, meal calendars, child care, marriage support, parenting support, fund-raising for the neighborhood and church, letter writing campaigns (right now to stop coal from being exported out of St. Helens, Oregon), lifestyle challenge, and support. One family generated only one can of garbage for the year; another stopped buying anything new for a year." Maria explained that the emphasis on simplicity and sharing resources allows nearly all community members to work less than full-time, providing more time to give to relationships and social action.

I asked about how they handle conflict and difference in community. Maria offered an example right away. "We don't always agree. For example, Last Thursday [a gallery open house and art festival in their NE Alberta neighborhood] is a contentious issue in our community. Some of us believe that it brings vitality to the area and makes it a lively, creative, dynamic place to live, or from a practical stance, without Last Thursday we would not have the economic redevelopment of the neighborhood. The event also represents an inclusive, diverse event. Others believe that it is a noisy, messy, potentially dangerous event that contradicts their family values. All of us are civically engaged, so our city council has received phone calls and emails from us representing all of these points of view."

I wondered how Friendship Community navigates such differences. Maria went on to share from her experience that it is a huge help for families not to share housing with each other. Living nearby but not in the same house creates enough space for difference. "When adults from different households live together, it's very difficult to allow differences in parenting, for example. When we have our own housing, differences are still a strain, but it doesn't feel as urgent to persuade one another to our way of thinking or doing things."

Maria described the importance of the spirit of grace, communication, struggle, and joy as themes that carry Friendship

Community forward and help them to navigate conflict and the daily realities of life together. "Sharing our lawn mowers, outdoor furniture, making a pot of soup and inviting everyone over, and helping tutor our community-mates' children are all experienced as generous gestures given and are received with grace and gratitude. When you live together in the same house, all these gestures are an expected part of helping out in a household. It can feel burdensome instead of grace-filled. When one Friendship Community family decided to only allow for one can of garbage for the year, it didn't produce conflict; it created admiration and the desire to imitate them. If we were a single, shared household, these decisions would need to be made in common.

"As for the Last Thursday conflict, we talk, and disagree, and encourage one another to email our city even though we disagree. I guess we have great sympathy for one another's point of view. We don't have to agree to understand the other point of view. I'd also say that we have a deep level of commitment to communication. Many of us have engaged in psychological and spiritual counseling, which gives us tools for communication. Our men's and women's groups have, as one of their purposes, sharing of feelings and processing experiences." Maria reflected on both challenges and blessings of life in Friendship Community. "Finding God in these everyday places is where we struggle and we experience joy."[5]

Some Big House and Friendship Community members are non-goers and others are highly committed to St. Andrew, their parish church. Together the communities they have forged outside the walls of the church have carried them forward, weathered the years, nurtured new generations, and continue to shape the daily life of community members and the lives of others around them. As non-goers, we can learn from this faithfulness and vision. We can be inspired, by their example, to find God and experience joy as we, too, embrace everyday challenges and ordinary blessings in committed community.

Springwater

I am regularly inspired and encouraged by Portland friends who make up Springwater Community. The community is named for its location near the Springwater trail in the low income Lents neighborhood in outer Southeast Portland. Serving on the Portland Parish Collective team with "Grassroots Storyteller and Field Guide" Brandon Rhodes, a member of Springwater, gives me the opportunity to hear stories of real community life in the Springwater neighborhood, hot off the press.

Asking for a ten-year commitment, a vow to live simply, and the willingness to move into the neighborhood, they launched in 2008 with twenty people in four houses. Rusty and Marylou Bonham, an empty-nester couple recently retired from pastoring in the Midwest, drew the group together. Most people didn't know each other when they started. As they all jumped in full of dreams and idealism, they learned quickly that the work of being in community with others is hard. An article featuring the community appeared in the *Oregonian* newspaper in 2011.

> "Some people weren't prepared for the intimacy required to live this way, for the intensity and frequency of their spiritual debates or simply having others within the church—virtual strangers in the beginning—hold them accountable for not biking often enough or not buying local. . . . Part of living in a community is learning to deal with people you don't necessarily agree with all the time," said Alison Hilkiah, who along with her husband was the first Springwater community member to move in. "Some of our monthly meetings were really tense. We had differences of opinion on everything. We didn't know each other well. We had all taken this big leap together without really knowing in a lot of cases what living communally actually means." . . . "Living in a community brings out the worst in a person. That's why we prefer it," Rusty Bonham said. "Our issues bubble to the surface, and that is where they can be dealt with."[6]

Over time some people have left, but others have stayed. They have established rhythms and practices to knit the group together and to continue growing spiritually. They welcome interns for shorter periods of time, and they are making their way forward. The community is made up of singles, young couples, new babies, and the Bonhams, who are in their fifties.

The community gathers for worship and to share "God sightings" from their week each Sunday afternoon. They each volunteer in some way to make the neighborhood a better place, and they all make time to hang out and get to know their neighbors. They are making a mark on the little corner of Lents they inhabit. Neighbors have come to trust them rather than wonder if they are a weird cult, which they did indeed wonder at first! Springwater friends have changed that impression by being themselves and reaching out.

They know how to throw a good party and welcome people in. They've rented the neighborhood pool and provided free admission for all, pulled the grill out into the driveway and put on not-to-be-missed barbecues and potlucks, made their couches available to people with nowhere else to go, planted gardens and shared veggies with neighbors, built sandboxes for neighborhood kids, held bike repair clinics, whacked blackberries back, and collected trash from the Springwater trail. The street looks brighter, cleaner, greener, and all neighbors know each other better. The neighborhood is slowly being transformed by friendship, and at the same time, as Brandon puts it, "I am being transformed in the process." With a lifespan of five years now, Springwater is halfway to the ten-year commitment. This is much further than many new church plants or intentional community start-ups manage to make it. Springwater intends to stay put much longer than ten years. They have begun to learn what a difference long-term commitment to friendship in one neighborhood can mean.

The life of the Springwater community, as a mix of singles, couples, and families, practices hospitality well together.

While communities and family groups might more easily facilitate hospitality for all, I know single people who have found their own ways to practice beautiful hospitality.

Michele, a friend who lives not far from me, is an excellent example. She always has an open bedroom for someone passing through town. At a time in this manuscript writing process when there was too much hubbub in my own house to concentrate, she gave me full use of a room in her house to use as a writing studio. I could slip away, leaving my own house, and write in peace. On many occasions she has made her spacious home available for me to throw an impromptu party or host an event when my own house was feeling small or messy. I know plenty of other single friends who may not have extra bedrooms, but their soft couches are open for people in need, and they are ready to share a bowl of soup or cup of tea anytime.

Brandon of Springwater married last year, but for several years was a twentysomething single guy in the community. Springwater life gave him the opportunity and the resources to be part of extending hospitality in natural ways as part of a community rather than as an individual. That has been one of the unexpected gifts of community for him.

Whether it is an extra bedroom, space on a couch, or a hot bowl of soup and a welcome at the table, communities with open doors and open hearts are needed in this world.

What Is Real

Every April, the Parish Collective Inhabit Conference takes place in Seattle. I was not present in 2013, but my Urban Abbey coleader Tamara was there. She returned to share with me that one of the most meaningful points of the conference was when Parish Collective and intentional community leader Tony Kriz stood before the people and shed the light of reality on the glorious stories that had been shared at Inhabit.

Speaking from his own experience, Tony told the conference attendees that this stuff is hard work. He told everyone that under no uncertain terms, building community involves grief and loss. He shared of community dreams that he and his wife, Aimee, held and worked hard for that hadn't panned out. As he spoke of their community of twenty people slowly dwindling down to just him, Aimee, and their two little boys, he let his tears flow. Tamara told me that Tony's honesty was more helpful to her than all the stories she'd heard at the conference about what was going right in communities. I asked Tony about this and he told me:

> That moment was a spontaneous moment. The stories from up-front had all been so triumphal (even when I know many of those communities and their very real struggles). I imagined all the people in the room who, like my wife, probably felt like they didn't have amazing things to share or stories to tell. I was suddenly afraid that they would somehow believe a lie that they do not belong in the room (in Parish Collective or even in the Kingdom) because they don't have triumphal stories. So I felt like it was important for someone in the spotlight to share another perspective.[7]

I am glad Tony followed that hunch and let the "real" show. I'd venture to say that the story and the feelings he shared mattered to many people at Inhabit. His words may matter to you too.

I return to the wisdom of Henri Nouwen: "You have to be willing to live your loneliness, your incompleteness, your lack of total incarnation fearlessly, and trust that God will give you the people to keep showing you the truth of who you are."[8] Those words certainly resonate with me. I know that we of Urban Abbey, we imperfect people, incomplete and lonely at times, have been given others who will keep showing us the truth of who we are. And as we do so, Jesus is with us.

May we all keep growing, continue learning, and become communities that bear light together, even in our brokenness.

And as you go forward wherever you find yourself, remember, you are not alone—others are on similar paths. This is hard work. It's okay to find closure. It's okay to make mistakes. It's okay to start simply.

The Power of Being Intentional

Inhabiting and loving abandoned neighborhoods, extending care for people in prisons, and investing in friendships in apartment complexes; building farms in crime-ridden, inner-city settings, creating community between neighbors who feel isolated and lonely in their homes and on their street, and living in shared houses or villages of proximity—whether single or family, intergenerational or an age affinity group, Roman Catholic or Protestant, connected to church or disconnected from church—we can remember that when it comes to intentional communities of Christ, "The call to radical discipleship is not a call to sameness."[9]

The stories of others can help to give perspective and let go of "shoulds" and "musts" and formulas. May shared stories seed hope for all of us as we make our way in this journey of following Jesus in community and in our neighborhoods.

❯❯ Questions and Action ❮❮

1. Historically, intentional, monastic, and neo-monastic communities tend to be renewal movements or responses to excess or neglect of the poor. What do you suppose is stirring the increasing number of intentional communities today?
2. Shane Claiborne says we should use our "imaginations to practice resurrection." What does that mean to you, right where you are?
3. Even if you aren't going to be in an intentional community, this chapter is packed with practical and creative

ideas for action and bringing good news. Go through this chapter and list those you can imagine doing.

4. Tony shared honestly about facing disappointment. Have there been times when you were helped by others honestly sharing about their "failure" and disappointments?

5. If you were in a community like the ones discussed in this chapter, what strengths would you bring to the community? What particular challenges would be most difficult for you?

14

CONCLUSION

All Said and Done and Just Beginning

Many more stories could be told. Some of those stories are yours—stories in process and stories yet to be lived.

You might be a non-goer well down the road of *being* church, you may be a non-goer who has been on your own a little too long, you may be a new non-goer wondering which way to turn, or you may be ready to leave church but are uncertain what that might mean. You may have tried long and hard and need to be blessed and told you are free to go.

If you do find it is time to go, I encourage you to go toward something rather than away from something. If you were wounded by the church and you've left in pain or discouragement, please, seek healing and don't allow that place of pain to settle in and take hold of you. Grieve, and when you are ready, move forward with the awareness that there is goodness to pursue. For those of you who have been lonely or uncertain, be encouraged that you are not the only one in this place of change. There is a place for you—make a way for others or seek out kindred souls for the way forward.

You may be a reader with the energy and vision to stay in the church and help others. For you goers with hopes for more in the church, for you goers who have enthusiasm and energy to continue on in your church congregation, and for you pastors with a call to a specific congregation—the epilogue, up next in this book, was written with you in mind. Wherever you stand at this time, I believe there is reason to be encouraged.

You are all invited on the amazing journey of joining with others in hopeful and powerful expressions of being church. The possibility of becoming part of healing and hope for a world hungry for visible images of Christ and for love incarnated is something you don't want to miss out on. Share with your neighbors, count ordinary attempts, don't go it alone—invite others. Keep studying and learning, bring others along, find mentors, rely on the Wild Goose—the Holy Spirit available to us all. Become aware of your own broken areas and seek personal transformation, welcome children, ask hard questions of yourself and then take action to answer them, play and savor life. In the spirit of sankofa, proceed with humility and respect for the history and investment of those who've paved the way to this point.

No matter where we are, we who choose to follow Jesus are each called to urge one another on to love and good deeds and to *be* church. Whichever way you are going, it's time to jump in and swim. Come on in, the water's fine.

EPILOGUE

An Open Letter to Churches

Dear Church,

Thank you for hanging in there in your own ministry, and thank you for your willingness to consider the stories this book contains. Let me make this clear: you are needed! I believe that you can be part of leading the shift from "going to church" to new, life-giving practices of "being church." With the guidance of the Holy Spirit, ears to hear what is needed today, and courage to put fear aside, the church, historically a powerful change agent for good in the world, could turn things upside down by divesting instead of holding on tight.

I hope the stories and voices of non-goers in this book may bring encouragement for your way forward. Creative and constructive evaluation of leadership structures and roles, building use, engagement with your neighborhood, church budgets, and pursuit of spiritual transformation are needed to meet the practical realities of this place in history. If you are willing to take risks for Jesus, I think you could lead the way—the world will be watching and drawn to Jesus as you do.

I've been thinking about the potential for the creation of renewing bodies within the larger church; "a church within a church" as one possible way forward. John Wesley saw the Methodist movement as a renewing force within Anglicanism.

As you've read, my own Third Saturday Community began and flourished as a church within a church for many years. What would happen if churches became home bases for many micro-communities of practice scattered around in neighborhoods and public places. Communities like this would be able to better know, understand, and be present to the people around them. Smaller, more flexible forms that do not depend on much financial support prepare the church to be more sustainable and to survive, thrive, minister, and adapt rapidly in times of economic change or national or ecological crisis.

Another bonus I see is that the role and quality of life for pastors may become healthier and more sustainable when churches find ways to genuinely equip the priesthood of all believers and make room for all the gifts in the church. Redistribute power and create safe spaces for people to raise questions and doubts. You'll retain potential leavers and, exponentially increase the relational impact of the ministry of the church.

I also know this is more easily said than done. Having invested a great deal of heart and love and care and work with the church plant in which my husband and I were dedicated lay leaders for twelve years, I do remember how discouraging it can feel when people leave. Shane Claiborne's wise reminder that "Jesus is not scared to see people walk away" would have been helpful for me to hear at a certain point in my own story. And, although Jesus may not be scared when people leave church, sometimes we are scared—or even hurt.

We are all treading unfamiliar waters—we may be holding on to old flotation devices or dog-paddling, depending on how far we've jumped, but we are all in this together. Churches and non-goers alike are called to a life of being church. It's worth repeating, no matter where we are, we who choose to follow Christ are each called to urge one another on to love and good deeds and to be church.

Courage, inspiration, and blessings as you explore what that looks like for you and your congregation.

With love, Kelly Bean

PERSONAL NOTE

August 13, 2013

Dear Reader,

As you may have figured out already, though I am a story-teller and I enjoy writing, I am really an activist and a prac-titioner at heart. That means that while this book was being crafted I was founding and cultivating communities, men-toring and discipling emerging leaders, living real life as a mom, wife, and friend—and yes, starting a nonprofit. What I've learned and where I've been in that process has certainly informed this book as it took shape.

When I began this book my children were nine, fifteen, and nineteen years old. Today, they are seventeen, twenty-three, and twenty-seven years old. The blessings of three grand-children have been added to the family in these eight years: Gabriel, seven; Abby Jane, one; and Kiana, two weeks.

These years have held blessings, and they've held real chal-lenges. To be clear about where I come from and how God has been at work, I am going for full disclosure. Never put others on a pedestal or think you know what's going on by looking at their Facebook wall or even reading their book.

We are all human and we all have real lives and real people in our lives. Until we make room to share the untidiness with authenticity, we won't be too appealing to real people around us. This is my real life, folks. And God is at work in it and in each one of us every day.

In 2006 my husband, Ken, was a top-producing Realtor. We lived in a spacious custom lodge we built ourselves out of reclaimed timbers on a small lake in the country. As self-employed people, we were accustomed to finances fluctuating, but our life was comfortable; we loved sharing what we had and we had leisure time to enjoy it. Our income came to a screeching halt with the 2008 economic downturn. For the next years we found ourselves floundering—digging for quarters in the car seats, gluing kids' shoe soles back on to make them last just a little longer, and taking on odd jobs to fill the gaps.

At the same time, even more painful than the strain of difficult finances was the journey of our young adult daughters. After high school both girls experimented with hard drugs and got hooked. I can come up with an assortment of explanations for their choices, but really, when it comes down to it, none of them make complete sense. Addiction is simply a terrible creature and disease. It was hell to watch our beautiful children on a path to destroying themselves. We did all we could to intervene and to get help. Eventually we came to realize that this was their journey and that our best response was to love them, pray, and take care of ourselves and our son. Their stories took us down roads we would never have imagined and taught us things we would never have signed up to learn.

Stressful is putting it mildly. Leisure time was not in the picture. Ken struggles with degenerative disk disease and lives with chronic pain. That rarely stops him completely, but when stress levels are high, the tension and pain escalate. That doesn't help life much either. To engage in the creative process under such circumstances was for me very trying. For several years, what was written was written in fits and starts.

Through these trials, our marriage has grown stronger, deeper, and more honest. Ken and I have battled adversity side by side, we've prayed feverishly into the wee hours, fought over differences of opinion, and loved each other for who we are in the middle of some tough times. I credit my husband for his unwavering faithfulness, his long-suffering optimism, his willingness to work his butt off, and his heart to make supportive space for me to pursue my call and my work in Rwanda and in leading community even in the middle of our trauma.

It was to a great degree a broad community of friends and family members from a variety of contexts in our lives that got us through this long haul. Urban Abbey friends pitched in with food and love and consistent prayer. Others shared vacation homes, paid for meals out, and showed us love in practical ways. An anonymous gift of a brand new guitar appeared for us to give to Elliot for Christmas one year when there was no money for presents. Friends actually gave to help with our house payments and lent us more when we were in a tight bind.

We have been blown away by love and real support. As supremely meaningful and helpful as the practical help with "stuff and money" has been, one of the greatest gifts for me has been true friends who have not grown weary of our trials. These friends have listened and listened and loved and prayed and listened some more. They are some of the most precious gifts in my life. Honestly, without this wealth of community and friendship, I am sure we would not have made it. I am not quite sure what not making it would have meant, but it wouldn't have been good. Without that circle of love, I know I would not have been able to continue forward in ministry and maybe not even in faith, and we certainly wouldn't still be in our home.

The economy is picking up, and though we are still catching up, we can breathe again. Today both of our daughters are clean and sober and are building new lives. They have wisdom and compassion born of trial. They are raising healthy children and returning to prayer and connection with the God of their childhood.

Prayer, poetry, and friends—all gifts from God—have carried me through the darkest of times and through these years of writing. I am learning and relearning how to live and trust one day at a time, and I find myself surprised by peace that passes understanding, even in the middle of great difficulty. Today I see the world through completely different eyes than I did eight years ago. All that we have seen and felt, whether or not we liked it, is now a valuable part of our story. We are not perfect people. We have not and will not always do things "right" or "best," but we live with hope, love, and deep gratitude for redemption.

We live as non-goers in supportive community. We live believing that our triune God is very present in all times and places. And we trust that the lessons we have learned from our stories will make us better able to be part of the story of the redemption of all things that Christ himself gave his life for.

With a grateful heart, Kelly

THE URBAN ABBEY STORY TEASER

Have you ever experienced going back three years in your personal journals and reading with the perspective of time? It can be interesting and insightful, to say the least. I invite you to join me in turning the pages to my story, written in 2010, as Urban Abbey began to form as a community. Then read on for the benefit and insight of time in part two, which was written in 2013. You can visit this online link for a free-of-charge, sneak-peek, behind-the-scenes look at the life story of Urban Abbey Intentional Community (as told and perceived by me of course). The first piece was based on a whole lot of hopes and enthusiasm held in 2010, depicting the community we were imagining and dreaming of. The second piece stands in the stark light of real life.

Without further ado, you are welcome to visit two bonus chapters of *How to Be a Christian without Going to Church* at www.howtobechristianwithoutgoingtochurch.com.

Get started with this bonus chapter teaser.

Once upon a time, a long, long time ago (the 1970s) in the small suburban burg of West Linn, Oregon, there was a dreamer. This dreamer imagined communities and housing where the old and the young, the brown and the white, the lonely and the overworked, found a home together. While some spent time going to homecoming dances, painting their nails, and sharing schoolgirl gossip, she sketched out designs for residential complexes where people would share gardens, kitchens, pets, and day-to-day life.

But she grew up and bought into a new dream: the American Dream. She married and had children, and she—with her husband—started a good business, joined a church, built a big house in the suburbs, worked hard to get more stuff and better stuff and to make sure that her children had every opportunity to learn. Even though she loved Jesus, served lunches to street people, and had thirty-four different people live with her family at one time or another, the dream began to feel hollow.

One fine day in 2006, the dreamer had a cup of coffee with a good friend and mentor. The mentor had been asking himself some questions too: In what ways have I become culturally captive to a Western, middle-class, consumer understanding of Christianity? How can I begin to break free from this to begin to live out the holistic gospel? They both agreed that such a re-orientation must be done with the support of a community of Christ-followers who were also willing to take such a journey. What if they were to uproot from the comfort and isolation of their suburban neighborhoods and gather others to form a transformative community?

Read on at www.howtobechristianwithoutgoingtochurch .com.

NOTES

Introduction

1. Kirk C. Hadaway and Penny Long Marler, "How Many Americans Attend Worship Each Week? An Alternative Approach to Measurement," *Journal for the Scientific Study of Religion* 44, no. 3 (September 2005): 307–22.

2. George Barna, *Revolution* (Wheaton, IL: Tyndale House, 2005), 13.

3. Craig Bird, "Pastor Says 'Post-Congregationals' Leaving Church, but Not Their Faith," *Associated Baptist Press* (October 30, 2002), http://www.rediscoveringchurch.com/leaving.asp.

4. Benton Johnson, Dean R. Hoge, and Donald A. Luidens, "Mainline Churches: The Real Reason for Decline," *First Things* (March 1993), http://www.firstthings.com/article/2008/05/001-mainline-churches-the-real-reason-for-decline-8.

5. Lovett H. Weems, "No Shows: The Decline in Worship Attendance," *Christian Century* (September 22, 2010), http://www.christiancentury.org/article/2010-09/no-shows.

6. NCC News Service, "Trends Continue in Church Membership Growth or Decline, Reports 2011 Yearbook of American & Canadian Churches," The National Council of the Church of Christ in the USA, New York (February 14, 2011), http://www.ncccusa.org/news/110210yearbook2011.html.

7. Eric Swanson and Rick Rusaw, *The Externally Focused Quest: Becoming the Best Church for the Community* (San Francisco: Jossey-Bass, 2010), 21.

8. Tim Stafford, "The Third Coming of George Barna," *Christianity Today*, August 5, 2002, http://www.christianitytoday.com/ct/2002/009/1.32.html.

Chapter 1 The Backstory

1. I am not exaggerating. The truth is, my father was a bona fide religious addict, which explains the unusual weekly field trips. Some families go to Yellowstone or to the art museum. We toured revivals and Sunday night special services.

2. A side note: now that I have been a parent of teens, I marvel at how co-operative I was, making all these shifts and going on so many church "family field trips."

3. See Deuteronomy 4:29.

4. Credit to "Arms Wide Open" by Creed, an inspiration during this time.

5. Andrei Rublev, *Icon of the Trinity*, 1410, http://www.wellsprings.org.uk/rublevs_icon/trinity.htm.

6. See Deuteronomy 4:29.

Chapter 2 What the Heck Is Church?

1. Jim Henderson and Matt Casper, *Jim & Casper Go to Church: Frank Conversation about Faith, Churches, and Well-Meaning Christians* (Carol Stream, IL: Barna Books, 2007), 147.

2. Luke 22:19.

3. Brian McLaren, Commencement Speech at Virginia Theological School, May 20, 2010, http://brianmclaren.net/archives/blog/commencement-address.html.

4. Matthew 18:20.

5. Leonard Sweet and Frank Viola, *Jesus Manifesto: Restoring the Supremacy and Sovereignty of Jesus Christ*, ebook (Nashville: Thomas Nelson, 2010), introduction.

6. Richard Rohr, a daily meditation from a Center for Action and Contemplation (CAC) email, adapted from *The Authority of Those Who Have Suffered*.

7. Richard Rohr, a daily meditation (August 24, 2009) from a CAC email, adapted from *The Authority of Those Who Have Suffered*.

8. McLaren, Commencement Speech.

9. Ryan Sharp, interview.

Chapter 3 Why Are People Leaving?

1. Alan Jamieson, *A Churchless Faith: Faith Journeys beyond the Churches* (London: SPCK, 2002), 2.

2. David Kinnaman and Gabe Lyons, *unchristian: What a New Generation Really Thinks about Christianity—and Why It Matters* (Grand Rapids: Baker, 2007), 40.

3. Julia Duin, *Quitting Church: Why the Faithful Are Fleeing and What to Do about It* (Grand Rapids: Baker, 2008).

4. In loving memory of Barbara Colburn, who passed away in 2013.

5. Edith Briggs, interview.

6. Gayle Wright, interview.

7. Jim Henderson, interview.

8. Barbara H. Henderson, "Simple Spirituality," 2002, http://www.offthemap.com/idealab/simple_spirituality_guide.pdf.

9. Amy, interview.

10. Dannika Nash, "An Open Letter to the Church from My Generation," www.dannikanash.com, April 7, 2013; http://dannikanash.wordpress.com/2013/04/07/an-open-letter-to-the-church-from-my-generation.

11. Robert D. Putnam and David E. Campbell, "Walking Away from Church," *Los Angeles Times,* October 17, 2010, http://articles.latimes.com/2010/oct/17/opinion/la-oe-1017-putnam-religion-20101017.

12. Benita Hewitt, "Church Attendance Has Bottomed Out," *The Guardian*, September 11, 2010, http://www.guardian.co.uk/commentisfree/belief/2010/sep/10/religion-christianity.

13. Dave Tomlinson, *The Post-Evangelical*, rev. North American ed. (El Cajon, CA: Emergent YS/Zondervan, 2003), 23.

14. Jamieson, *A Churchless Faith*, 53.

15. Ibid.

16. Ibid., 79, 84.

17. Ibid.
18. Ibid., 94, 95, 102.
19. Ibid, 15.
20. Ibid., 42.
21. Ibid., 103.
22. Arnie Chupp, interview.
23. David G. Benner, *Spirituality and the Awakening Self: The Sacred Journey of Transformation* (Grand Rapids: Brazos, 2012), 175.
24. Philip Jenkins, *The Next Christendom: The Coming of Global Christianity* (New York: Oxford University Press, 2002).
25. Soong-Chan Rah, *The Next Evangelicalism: Releasing the Church from Western Cultural Captivity* (Downers Grove, IL: IVP, 2009).
26. Elizabeth Dias, "The Latino Reformation: Inside the New Hispanic Churches Transforming Churches in America," *Time*, April 15, 2013, http://www.nhclc.org/en/news/time-latino-reformation. See also http://nation.time.com/2013/04/the-rise-of-evangelicos.

Chapter 4 What Are They Doing Now?

1. Jamieson, *A Churchless Faith*, 102.
2. Ibid.
3. Leonard I. Sweet, *Post-Modern Pilgrims: First Century Passion for the 21st Century World* (Nashville: Broadman & Holman, 2000), 33.
4. Ibid., 142.
5. Ibid., 86.
6. Ibid., 86.
7. Ibid., 109–10.
8. Ibid., 131.
9. Ibid., 117.
10. Desmond Tutu, Naomi Tutu, ed., *The Words of Desmond Tutu: Second Edition* (New York: Newmarket Press, 2006), back cover.

11. Sweet, *Post-Modern Pilgrims*, 117.
12. Diana Butler Bass, *Christianity after Religion: The End of Church and the Birth of a New Spiritual Awakening* (New York: HarperOne, 2012), 66, 68.
13. Philip Goldberg, "Spiritual but Not Religious: Misunderstood and Here to Stay," Huffington Post Religion Blog, February 2, 2013, http://www.huffingtonpost.com/philip-goldberg/spiritual-but-not-religious-misunderstood-and-here-to-stay_b_2617306.html.
14. SBNR.org via Mike Morrell, "Jesus and Religion's Relationship Status—It's Complicated," January 18, 2012, http://www.huffingtonpost.com/mike-morrell/jesus-and-religions-relationship-status_b_1213243.html.
15. Benner, *Spirituality and the Awakening Self*, 174.

Chapter 5 Face-to-Face

1. Romans 15:5–7 ESV.
2. "The Aims and Means of the Catholic Worker," http://www.catholicworker.org/aimsandmeanstext.cfm?Number=5.
3. Christian Reflection by Center for Christian Ethics. Study guide for Coleman Fannin, "Dorothy Day's Radical Hospitality," Christian Reflection: A Series in Faith and Ethics. 2007. http://www.baylor.edu/content/services/document.php/53393.pdf.
4. Arnie Chupp, interview.
5. Adapted from "Finding Mentors: Building a Mentoring Constellation," by Terry B. Walling. Downloadable PDF Resource. Leader Breakthru University, http://www.leaderbreakthru.com/lbu/catalog.php?action=view_product&id=24. Also in Focused Living Resource Kit by Terry Walling. Churchsmart Resources, 1999.

Chapter 6 God with Us

1. Troy Bronsink, *Drawn In: A Creative Process for Artists, Activists, and Jesus Followers* (Brewster, MA: Paraclete Press, 2013), 102.
2. Ibid., 144.
3. Charlie Peacock, interview.
4. Dmitri Siegel, "Designing Our Own Graves," in *Graphic Design Theory: Readings from the Field*, ed. Helen Armstrong (New York: Princeton Architectural Press, 2009), 115.
5. Allison Aubrey, "How the DIY Butter Trend Got Churning," *All Things Considered*, July 4, 2013, http://www.npr.org/blogs/thesalt/2013/07/04/198425906/how-the-diy-butter-trend-got-churning?utm_source=atc&utm_medium=facebook&utm_campaign=20130704.
6. Kathy Escobar, *Down We Go: Living into the Wild Ways of Jesus* (Folsom, CA: Civitas Press, 2011), 81.

Chapter 7 Hands On

1. Nathan Lommasson, interview.
2. Andrew Jones, interview.
3. http://www.globeaware.org.
4. Edward Simiyu, interview.

Chapter 8 Alternatives

1. Dennis Linn, Sheila Fabricant Linn, and Matthew Linn, *Sleeping with Bread: Holding What Gives You Life* (Mahwah, NJ: Paulist Press, 1995).
2. Shane Claiborne, Jonathan Wilson-Hartgrove, and Enuma Okoro, *Common Prayer: A Liturgy for Ordinary Radicals* (Grand Rapids: Zondervan, 2010).
3. Mypheduh Films, *Sankofa*, http://spot.pcc.edu/~mdembrow/sankofa.htm.
4. "What Is the Meaning of Sankofa," tribe.net, May 9, 2007, http://people.tribe.net/ac179361-11f7-4349-af25-ee8e502b9f68/blog/4d4a9874-325d-4239-9ef0-d3f1bc4ffcb5; "Sankofa," University of Illinois, Springfield, http://www.uis.edu/africanamericanstudies/students/sankofa.html
5. Paul Vitello, "Taking a Break from the Lord's Work," *New York Times*, August 1, 2010, http://www.nytimes.com/2010/08/02/nyregion/02burnout.html?pagewanted=all.
6. http://www.pastorburnout.com.
7. Andy Crouch, "Planting Deep Roots: When You Get Serious about Cultural Change, You Get Serious about Institutions," *Christianity Today*, July 11, 2013, http://www.christianitytoday.com/ct/2013/june/why-we-love-institutions-planting-deep-roots.html?paging=off. Note: one year later Bell left his role of founding pastor and assumed a ministry role in a less institutional setting.

Chapter 9 Money, Money, Money

1. "Triple Bottom Line," *Economist*, November 17, 2009, www.economist.com/node/14301663.
2. http://thearborlodge.com/#ethos.
3. http://theoregoncommunity.com.
4. http://oregonpublichouse.com.
5. http://www.ecomopeds.com.

Chapter 10 Without the Container

1. Diana Butler Bass, *Christianity for the Rest of Us: How the Neighborhood Church Is Transforming the Faith* (San Francisco: HarperSanFrancisco, 2006).
2. Hebrews 10:24–25.
3. http://www.swarthmore.edu/libraries/beit-midrash.xml.
4. http://www.myjewishlearning.com/texts/Rabbinics/Midrash/Midrash_Aggadah/How_Midrash_Functions/

Midrash_Today.shtml. Excerpted with permission from *Searching for Meaning in Midrash* (Jewish Publication Society).

5. Micah D. Halpern, "The Art of Debate: Jewish Style," http://asiasociety.org/countries/religions-philosophies/art-debate-jewish-style.

6. http://www.tierra-nueva.org/The PeoplesSeminary.html.

7. Chris Hoke, interview. Hoke's forthcoming book with HarperCollins will share accounts of how his life was changed as he was befriended by inmates.

8. Matthew 22:8–10.

9. Matthew 22:11–14.

10. Doug Pagitt, *Preaching Re-Imagined: The Role of the Sermon in Communities of Faith* (Grand Rapids: Zondervan, 2005), 44.

11. http://worship.calvin.edu/grants/urban-hymnal.

12. Ibid.

13. Ibid.

14. Brother Roger, in Jason Brian Santos, *A Community Called Taizé: A Story of Prayer, Worship and Reconciliation* (Downers Grove, IL: IVP, 2008), 63.

15. "In More Depth," http://www.moot.uk.net/about/in-more-depth.

16. Ibid.

17. Steve Collins, "A Definition of Alternative Worship," 2012, http://www.alternativeworship.org/definitions_definition.html.

18. Ibid.

19. http://www.alternativeworship.org.

20. http://www.visions-york.org/Welcome.html.

Chapter 11 Alt–Sunday School and Alt–Youth Group

1. Mark Yaconelli, "Less Talk, More Action," http://www.patheos.com/Topics/Passing-on-the-Faith/Less-Talk-More-Action-Mark-Yaconelli-08-02-2013.html.

2. Mark Scandrette, *Free: Spending Your Time and Money on What Matters Most* (Downers Grove, IL: IVP, 2013), 73.

Chapter 12 Parish Is Hip

1. Raymond J. Bakke, *A Theology as Big as the City* (Downers Grove, IL: IVP, 1997), 60.

2. Alan Hirsch, "Defining Missional," *Christianity Today/Leadership Journal*, Fall 2008, Dec. 12, 2008, http://www.ctlibrary.com/le/2008/fall/17.20.html.

3. Ibid.

4. Escobar, *Down We Go*, 50.

5. Ibid., 51.

6. Ibid., 83.

7. Lesslie Newbigin, *The Gospel in a Pluralist Society* (Grand Rapids: Eerdmans, 1989, 2002), 233.

8. Steve Knight, "A Must-See for Missional Christians," November 23, 2012, http://www.patheos.com/blogs/missionalshift/2012/11/a-must-see-for-missional-christians.

9. Shauna Niequist, "How One Woman Created a Community Out of a Neighborhood," *Storyline* blog, January 30, 2013.

10. Darrell L. Guder, ed., *Missional Church: A Vision for the Sending of the Church in North America* (Grand Rapids: Eerdmans, 1998), 177.

11. Aurora Commons, "About Us," 2012, http://www.auroracommons.org/aboutus.

12. Michelle Boorstein, "Activist DC Church Embraces Transition in Name of Its Mission," *The Washington Post*, January 6, 2009, http://articles.washingtonpost.com/2009-01-06/news/36840532_1_social-justice-christmas-service-church.

13. Ibid.

14. Ibid.

15. Chris Young, "How to Improve Pedestrian Safety in Your Neighborhood," Neighborhood Notes, February 28, 2012, http://www.neighborhood notes.com/news/2012/02/how_to_im prove_pedestrian_safety_in_your_ neighborhood.

16. City Repair, "The Vision of City Repair," http://cityrepair.org.

17. Ibid.

18. Ibid.

19. Paul Sparks, interview.

20. http://www.pri.org/stories/busi ness/social-entrepreneurs/cash-mobs-profit-locally-owned-stores-8498.html.

Chapter 13 Intentional Communities

1. Dietrich Bonhoeffer, *Discipleship* (Minneapolis: Fortress, 2003), 46.

2. Dorothy Day, *All the Way to Heaven: The Selected Letters of Dorothy Day* (New York: Random House, 2012), 457.

3. "Aristides, AD 137," in Dave Blundell, *Hungry for Life: A Vision of the Church That Would Change the World* (Nashville: WestBow Press, 2010), 62.

4. Steve Collins, "A Definition of Alternative Worship."

5. Maria Fleming, interview in person and via email.

6. Anna Griffin, "Couple Live Their Faith by Building Community in Southeast Portland's Lents Neighborhood," *Oregonian*, July 7, 2011, http://www.oregonlive.com/news/oregonian /anna_griffin/index.ssf/2011/07/couple_ live_their_faith_by_bui.html.

7. Tony Kriz, interview.

8. Henri J. M. Nouwen, *The Inner Voice of Love: A Journey through Anguish to Freedom* (New York: Doubleday, 1996), 54.

9. Shane Claiborne, interview.

Catch up with
community cultivator, speaker,
and social activist

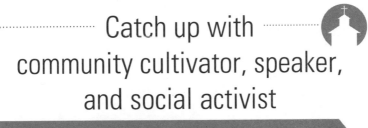

KELLY BEAN

at **kelly-bean.com**

Connect with

Sign up for announcements about new and upcoming titles at

www.bakerbooks.com/signup

 ReadBakerBooks

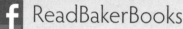 ReadBakerBooks